MISCHIEF NIGHT

Roddy Lumsden's first book *Yeah Yeah Yeah* (Bloodaxe Books, 1997) was shortlisted for Forward and Saltire first book prizes. His second collection *The Book of Love* (Bloodaxe Books, 2000), a Poetry Book Society Choice, was shortlisted for the T.S. Eliot Prize. *Mischief Night: New & Selected Poems* (Bloodaxe Books, 2004) draws on these two books as well as *Roddy Lumsden is Dead* (Wrecking Ball Press, 2001), a new collection, *The Drowning Man*, his pamphlet *The Bubble Bride*, and a previously uncollected sonnet sequence, *Cavali Riscaldati*.

He is a freelance writer, specialising in quizzes and word puzzles, and has held several residencies, including ones with the City of Aberdeen, St Andrews Bay Hotel, and in 1999 as "poet-in-residence" to the music industry when co-wrote *The Message*, a book on poetry and pop music published by the Poetry Society. He co-edited *Anvil New Poets 3* (2003) with Hamish Ironside. In 2004 Chambers Harrap publish his popular reference book *Vitamin Q: a temple of trivia, lists and curious words*. Born in St Andrews in 1966, he lived in Edinburgh for several years before moving to London.

Mischief
Night

NEW & SELECTED POEMS

RODDY LUMSDEN

BLOODAXE BOOKS

ISBN: 1 85224 672 3

First published 2004 by
Bloodaxe Books Ltd,
Highgreen,
Tarset,
Northumberland NE48 1RP.

www.bloodaxebooks.com
For further information about Bloodaxe titles
please visit our website or write to
the above address for a catalogue.

Bloodaxe Books Ltd acknowledges
the financial assistance of
Arts Council England, North East.

Cover printing by J. Thomson Colour Printers Ltd, Glasgow.

Printed in Great Britain by
Cromwell Press Ltd, Trowbridge, Wiltshire.

for Betty, Hamish, Jimmy, Carol, Eric, Rachel,
Mhairidh, Eilidh, Jim and Katie:
all Lumsdens and all loved.

ACKNOWLEDGEMENTS

This book includes poems from the following collections: *Yeah Yeah Yeah* (Bloodaxe Books, 1997), *The Book of Love* (Bloodaxe Books, 2000), *Roddy Lumsden Is Dead* (Wrecking Ball Press, 2001) and *The Bubble Bride* (St Andrews Bay, 2003).

Acknowledgements are due to the editors of the following publications where some of the previously unpublished poems first appeared: ACE International Fellowship brochure, *Chapman*, *ibid*, *Love for Love* (pocketbooks, 2000), *PBS Bulletin*, Poetry International brochure, *Poetry* (USA), *Poetry Review*, *The Reater*, *The Red Wheelbarrow*, *Rising*, *Scratch*, *The Wolf*; and to the following websites: *Frank's Casket* (dspace.dial.pipex.com/town/walk/xen19), *nthposition* (www.nthposition.com), *Scottish Art Council Poem of the Month* (www. scottisharts.org.uk), *Snakeskin* (www.snakeskin.org.uk) and *the poem* (www.thepoem.co.uk).

I would like to thank the Arts Council of England for an International Fellowship in Banff, Canada where some of the new work was written and also Arts & Business, StAnza Poetry Festival and the St Andrews Bay Golf Resort and Spa for the residency during which several poems here were written. For help with recent work, I wish to thank Julia Copus, A.B. Jackson, Kathleen Ossip, Joanna Quinn, John Stammers and Todd Swift. I would like too to express my gratitude to all those who have given advice and support during the fifteen years spanned by the work in this book.

CONTENTS

from **RODDY LUMSDEN IS DEAD** (2003)

Roddy Lumsden Is Dead

THE DROWNING MAN

Who swims in sin shall sink in sorrow.

PROVERB

I'm doing all right, feeling fine, still alive, I'm doing all right, feeling fine, I'm doing all right, I'm still alive, I'm doing fine!

MARQUIS DE SUAVE, *Postcards*

The Tremendous Few

So many, so many songs
    for the suicides, for the lives
docked in middle age;
    those taken in the evening's hiss

or who buckle in the draught
    halfway across the ford.
When the day tarries, I wonder
    if only you and I whisper

of scattered ashes, shoebox coffins,
    the gemstone hearts
of the stillborn and miscarried
    who did not reach the shore,

whose fading voices fail to split
    the hanging dark
when children throng the streets
    in gangs on Mischief Night.

Charcoal Sketch

Fire on the fields – the stubble
sputters and the larksong stops
in mid-note. The chapel bell
creaks on in the evening haze.

Turmoil in the henhouse
while in the barton, lentils
spill from a toppled, airtight
flagon and tick onto the table.

A cigar snivels in a jamjar.
Craneflies jig on the sap.
A rusting boneshaker merges
with the coalshed's copper roof.

The charcoal burner prods
his parched heap to make amends.
His compass needle spins
in mayhem; he sucks a sweet root.

Down in the hideout, two curly-
headed tykes practise hand jive
or else the sinister language
which the hand jive has become.

What Love Cannot Do

It could not save my friend from seeing what a window
showed him one night, it was Christmas, can't slow
the wave that swallowed Noel, Nelly beneath the wheel,
the bad seed in Ruth's little breast, *girls when they fall,*

won't castigate the squeeze who plumps for greedy sex
behind your back, our families picked off like tin ducks,
the daft bear galloping from side to side to side;
my rock thuds down again on the sick gull's head,

my rock, six kitties hanging from a rowan branch
and no you will not catch it cancelling a flint, a flinch,
the jailer's giggling stun gun, wire in my belly;
love lugs and struggles upstream, love is only holy,

it does not suckle, wears no fur, will leave no prints;
quit bolstering it, honey, here's my evidence:
when meat rains, when meat rains from the sky,
accept it, love will not be hovering nearby.

Miss Hollington's Notes

* a chorus of rum babas heaving preposterously behind cold glass * the trophy smears when hot fudge lifts from greaseproof paper * a squadron of traybakes awaiting rosettes * the sottish way I feel with my tongue lodged in a tub of clotted cream * the crevice in a blackcurrant boiling sharp enough to slice a cheek * brandy butter lurching down my leg at half a mile an hour * a gugglet of crème de banane to make me loll * a salvo of sweet-water grapes * the tongue chancing on cold sherbet in the belly of a raspberry blob * a bear-paw mapped with maple sap * the life rattle of coated raisins in a little tin * the lazy Susan spinning laden swooning * a currency of wild berries dipping over the sluice * Josiah's Bay Float supped from a half pineapple * my silly dream-face slick with nectar * the syrupy crumbs of Kugelhopf, jalousie and lingue di gatto * a kaleidoscope punnet of hundreds and thousands * a dowager duchess's wig of candy floss * the sweet shoots which the pygarg nips in Genesis *

Us

The usual entertainments. The brazen tune
of sticks along a fence. The silt of hunger.
Ablution's waltzes; the neat bolt well-oiled
on the door-back. A collie pup moping
on the smell of onion gravy. The bell-pull
lurching as we dip into the corner shop
for cheddar cheese or toffees or green soap.
Solid stuff. Our pith and quintessence.
The saga of our neighbour's leaning shed.
A tinfoil square on the grill. Adrift, a pool
of coppers in an ashet. Us. A red rosette
on a jelly jar. Milk snuffling in a pan.
The wooden rule suspended on a nail.
The sewing tin. Tinned salmon. Those who can.

Q

...too many able fires...

TORI AMOS, 'Doughnut Song'

A pupil of resilience, today I realign
myself as leg or breast man, canvassing
the campuses, the city parks and concourses
for waist-length plaits or teeming lips

although I know that only your eyes
(before I knew you, yes, and when and since)
work me thorough. Puzzling and brilliant,
as pretty in your diamond tomboy moments

as the drizzle nights you put the damage on
and as pretty then as on a New York corner
outside the Ukrainian diner, back when
my solid kissing still made a puddle of you,

holding you hard to me, against all weather,
our hearts pulsing as quick then and as close
as the future was, our splendid, awful future
surging ahead of us, a runaway.

Rain at Night

Since you ask, lass, this is how I get to sleep:
I've imagined a string of numbered planets
which loop and dip out towards the husk
of our universe; pretended to be a wren
tucked in a leaf, safe from the peril of sleet;

or better still, I pictured myself as a buck
in a burrow, and stroked your bible head,
my young love, doused there in your slumber,
the way he'd shush his trembling kits. Did
I mention how much I wish I was a father?

But mostly I think of these two: the couple
recording rain at night, my champions.
He is on one knee, a microphone in hand
held up as an offering to chance and weather
while she leans over, fluttering her level.

They must, since we must, have the sound
of rain. Rain drifting, becoming silver
and manifest above the churchyard, spun down
on flower fields and rockpools, spattering panes
of the watchman's hut while a wet cat

shudders home. And my champions remain
solid in their task, unnamed, known only to me
until, sleepless without you, I whispered this,
as if you hear me across the noise of rain,
the darkened counties dropping off, the emptiness.

The Knack

No Restoration comedy
in the eye of the squirrel;
        no ballerinas practise
on those distant lava slopes.
        Stage Left, Stage Right –
who could point those out
        in these palaces of cloud?
And yet when, drawn by music,
        I thrust my arm
down into the cold, black pond,
        you held on.

The Waitresses

And if your faith should waver
or shrieking harbour birds awaken
you from slumber in a lather;
should you then wonder
whether I am worth the bother, think
how much worse it might be:

that Bournemouth widow drunk
on the voice of the speaking clock,
or those two sisters outside Cattistock
church hall, false-lashed and lipsticked,
awaiting the annual visit
of the knock-kneed organ tuner;

the moon-eyed teen with her ear to the river
or the crone in the cave whose crooning sailor
(*we* know, *she* doesn't) will never
now march back across that shaking sea.
Three months isn't such a long time, is it,
to wait for me?

Sorry

When I hurt you and cast you off, that was buccaneer work:
the sky must have turned on the Bay that day and spat.
We'd tarried on corners, we'd dallied on sofas, we were
in *progress*, do you see? Yet stormcloud bruises bloomed

where once we touched. The walls swam under minty fever;
we failed to reach the long, low sleep of conquerors.
Since I played wrong and you did too, since *we* were wrong,
we need apologies; for your part in this sorry slip of hearts,

you should walk on Golden Hill at night alone; for mine
I will hang with my enemies, out on the long shore,
our brigand bodies impaled on the thorns of our failures,
the cold day casting draughts through our brinkled bones.

Life Story

Because I'd served the devil *and* the lord,
I rode home late, taking my care to shun
the known fact and the lost art and the word.
The night was not my own and in the dawn,

I stepped out and the world was not familiar,
the day, a cold ceramic on a shy
just beyond the clutches of my fingers
and framed against the fine skins of the sky.

Moments of Terror

Ladies, gentlemen, raise your glasses
in honour of small moments of horror:
the black lie eavesdropped, the battery

near-dead in the alarm you sleep through,
the lover glimpsed in the grasp of another,
for these gaunt things redeem us

in their awful properness, cleansing:
the systematic ticking, the advance
of sorry letters and of telltale stains,

the key in mid-air drops towards the drain,
lost footings, blind bends appearing
on the night road. Raise three cheers

for the agent provocateur punching the air,
for the ugsome stranger who wakes beside you,
nameless, with hairy hands and heavy breathing,

for why did we heave with our fins and gasp
and leave the swamp, if not to hear
the porch door creak, the strangler on the stair.

Fear of Music
(NYC, 1979)

The discothèque has closed, all the discos
barred and shuttered, yes, the bumping done,
the coloured cocktail glasses stamped on
and the bulbs beneath the dancefloor blown;
men of age, their faces composed by cocaine,
stand cooked in alleys in Chinese leather shoes;
police, pouting beneath New Wave haircuts,
square the downtown blocks in unmarked cars.

The parties are over – a blue smoke will lull
the bathhouse. Skirts succumb below the knee,
nipples are ice-cubed. Cigars no longer sell.
A gaunt guy sets off in a borrowed hearse
to discover Brooklyn. Boys and girls in bedrooms
gaze hard into themselves, find wanting
the wanton recent. Guns are something.
Guns *are* something. Itching rhythms burst.

And bombs fall from the air. At first,
just someone shooting – disaster movies –
and then it's fireworks, crystal rivers
over Queens; squibs light lowlit Harlem.
The delis throb and pizzerias prosper
selling poor man's mirrors – stoners stare down
dinner then, when a neon cowboy casts his hat out
over Times Square, a chill wind from the Steppes

strafes those still trying to imagine Heaven:
an orchard, stripped, where ideals wheel,
uncatchable, in twister winds. The future ends.
Our future ends! These ghetto preachers whip
the black book. WASP geeks spin a quarter bit
which comes down tails and Wall Street banks
whisper of *deep code*, brokers whisper zeal.
Fear of music in Village dives. Up in the Bronx,

the Zoo toils – animals make bad examples.
Stifling under breeze block, toughened glass,
our bleating impersonators stumble round.
Penguins stand in line to leave the man-made ice;
snakes are ideas above their station; the giddy lion
yawns and dreams himself upon a stool, sinks
a PBR in a smoky, foodless bar and, at last,
the sound of the jungle bursts in from the street.

Second Prayer

(after Polina Barskova)

Gaze down this way, Lord, send us down some pity
as sulphur moon spins out towards translucent night
for I've gone blank on how it came to this:
my friend and I sunk in silence, scraping the dregs
from a Nestlé's milk can with an apostle spoon,
a family heirloom, while over on the Avenue, the tram
thunders then throbs then thrums into the distance.
Or how it came to this now: dressed up fat in layers,
we wander through the Garden, bawling down
the grinning dog whose keen eyes seek the duck
leading her cavalcade of little ones; or how,
skirting the mesh-fence along the canal's brink,
fumbling past each other in the autumn dark,
my life seems a copy of your own, a tribute, bespoke.
We're free at last to joke about the others
who held us once, their faces indistinct, their names,
their very names a jumble. And we joke about the dead
who left us here, abandoned us to... what?
Not hurry. See the kettle puffing on its ring of heat,
cheese toppling from the slab, bread from the loaf.
We open the master's book at the longest poem.
The dog closes her lids, kicks, re-runs the walk;
out there, floodwater feeds the river's fever.

For Jesus

Dusk, outskirts of Calgary. I've just smoked five figurados
down to the jip to get my voice low enough to sing this.
True light makes its last moves on the fields. One bite left
of an oaten cookie, pudgy and viscid, its good dough flesh,
white choc chunks. She's flying back and my left eye binds
and binds the stress of sorrow. Here, where day roads end,

I press my *digitus impudicus* to thick, coach-window glass.
Ah glass! I hate the way *the way we touched* withers to less
now she is in the sky. Soon, pour me off a pint of Arctic Red
with Rich Tea sweetness and bitter fuss, shore bubble head
and forgive me, my snowboarding barman, I have my reasons
when I leave the last half copper inch of it *for Jesus*.

It's only a ploy in my endgame. A draught above heat
above snow on snow, to take me back to where desire operates:
the iceblind gulch between what's wanted and what hurts.
Listen, my bonny aproned boy. Write down these words.
Before I go, you'll need them, to remind me. You will now
Won't you? *The prettier they are the deader they kill you.*

Letter from an Admirer

Dear Mr Lumsden, your mention in a poem
of *loveless marriage* sang out to me, but instead
shall I mention how a hooded crow
makes both dining-chair and dinner of a lamb's head,

that fat house spiders will gestate in a schoolboy's ear,
how the frogfish awaits its prey, nine hours, stone-still,
that the red-eyed hyena, padding dust on a trail,
has a conscience that swings between zero and nil.

The Bath in Milk

The sleep-thief lust keeps us up
all the mischief hours; we warm
gallons of it, pans brimming,

the kettle thudding, the oven
frothing with flagons. Four AM
and you're waist-deep, dizzy

on its animal smell, my hands
caramelising on your breasts.
I write up our code-word –

L*** – in the filmy steam
misting the full-length mirror.
Your green eyes ghost over.

Lean back, lean back and smoulder.

The Drowning Man

Ambition knocks – a tropical disease.
My voice now slows and comes at you
as if through a wave of coconut milk.
The lifeboat glugs into a world of rust.
The wind eccentric quiets the blue
above my head, over our heads.

In the elsewhere, I see majorettes, the ends
of rummage sales, the heaving panther
coiling round an oak, I think I see
a dim light from a forest shack, I think I see
the outline of an arm through tinted glass,
my children sliding down the sky, not born.

Between Hallowe'en and Bonfire Night

Just then, encountering my ruddy face
in the grand piano's cold, black craquelure,
it conjured the jack-o'-lantern moon
dipping up over the roofs of the Tenderloin.

Only when I have done with the myths –
the inner spill that triggers us to flame,
breasts so sensitive a moment's touch
will call down fever; the dark sea-lane

between limbic squall and the heart's harbour –
will I picture you, just beyond innocence,
lying stripped by a thrown-wide window,
letting the cool breeze covet your ardour.

The Deaths of Imaginary Friends

They don't go easily and Mum still sets
the extra place a week after you hoist
the black flag to announce the sudden death
by bushfire, bomb or tiger teeth.

Still, wisps of fish and waxy, ketchup-stained
spuds sneak off the plate; you look outside –
a Matchbox Porsche roars across the drying yard;
that whisking in the berry patch is not the wind.

Their chippy hearts turn douce, their gimcrack souls
shudder on empty and when, arms linked, you swan
with a real child, it's then they long for caramel,
your scolding, and Master Bun the Baker's Son.

And though the puppy names you gave embarrass them,
that's all they have, as they huddle on the quayside,
waiting for the ship you promised would arrive,
a ship they are sure will come.

Moments of Pleasure

When those who had died
    as I shall soon
step forward in my memory
    one conclusive time,
the wall slumps down
    and calm gems,
glittering within, inherit me;
    for my intent, you see,
was never to attract,
    instead hang back
to see where I was drawn,
    the thrown boy, amplified
by night and by the place
    my name had been
without me, whispering, *now, yes.*

Still

How quiet these sealess hours
while you are gone, breaking the news.
A cat spooked by its own shadow
has become its own statue;

up in a third floor window
I stand without a flicker
while in this tumblerful of orange
not one bubble ticks. Yet both the drink

and the glass itself are liquids
and, given an age, would perform the trick
of becoming one. There in the fridge,
a block of Cheddar acts cold and thick

and yet it teems with pirouetting germs,
a little zoo. And though I do not seem to move,
my heart keeps time till your return –
and us, still quick into each other's arms.

Turning into Grizzly Street

That's what I'm like, like someone whistling
    'Yellow Bird' or 'Yankee Doodle',
stomping home beneath the Northern
    lights a-shining – *Heeeere's Roddy!*
Fifteen below and no hat with me:
    bald as gulls' eggs, Yul and Telly,
my tummy full and all the trimmings,

    Reese's Cups and crabmeat chowder,
Arctic Red; like someone crooning
    'A Case of You' or 'Chelsea Morning'
by Joni (who was born Roberta);
    oh Canada, how cold, how dry –
you make of me Orion skulled,
    the guest star in a winter drama,

the brown king on the second camel,
    and never a word is dithered or dull.
What am I like? Unhinged, unsteady,
    up Caribou Street, onto Grizzly,
my big feet sinking down through powder,
    the gardens jaunting below their blankets
all white and crispy. I've gone troppo,

    let's make that *frosto*, log cabin fever.
Tunnel Mountain hovers neatly;
    the air runs so thin, I get jealous.
As scabby cougars, scrawny coyotes
    circle the township, hot springs bubble
in Electric Shock and Nosebleed City.
    If it ain't beef it ain't Alberta.

Are those the songs of Cassin's auklet,
    tundra swan and purple martin?
That's what I'm like, like a lone elk nosing
    for fronds in the topfreeze, a nutcracker squat
on a creaking lodgepole. Stars fizz for me,
    the man-in-the-moon hawks out a comet,
night gets giggles, the world tastes funny.

From the Valentine Studio

(near Banff, Alberta)

The little three-holed Bakelite sockets here resemble dubious alien faces or Hallowe'en masks for finches. By the age of thirty-five, you have garnered enough emotional armour to deal with the simulacra of near-faces asking 'Who the hell are you?', but above the towel rail in the toilet, there is a pair of them and a second opinion is something you only ever claim with the voice of dread droning on your shoulder.

*

On the tatty cover of this Arvo Pärt CD I've borrowed in a misguided effort to better myself, 'An den Wassern zu Babel' is rendered as 'An den Wassern zu Babe!' Why is it that when I encounter evidence that I have a nook in this world, it always shows its face in the guise of misprints or, even more satisfying, in the international currency of downright lies?

*

Which one would you choose, I demand of myself, knowing no one in the busy late night campus bar. And I opt for the obvious one: a French style brunette in a denim waistcoat, who can't weigh more than eight stones. I wouldn't look twice at her normally, unless she was reading the news of my forthcoming hanging. But this is a foreign country. I don't want my tastes billowing about me like a bad flag, even for my own self to see.

*

Fresh cougar tracks are found at the bridge along the way. A cross-country skier has been eaten not so long ago. I skirt back to the hut hearing each of the dark's wiles and creaks. I'm not resolved to being hunted – it has less allure than a punctured lung. Nature so far means the robin on the tattie shaw, sad eyed kye resting their necks on the dry stane dyke. But then what does being hunted dispassionately count for in this season of sideshow slaughter and phantom battles?

*

Yet another girl wearing her wool hat indoors, which shows off how much and how well she is smiling. Why can't I have someone who smiles, I implore, before remembering that all my loves have been smiley and crisp. It's me who is the problem.

*

Listening to the Six Nations Women Singers, an Iroquois vocal combo, I marvel at the breadth of their subject matter. The first song is about the White Man's destruction of mother earth, the second about frittering cash on bingo. Six nations, though? The world continues to smither into fractions. It crosses my mind that somewhere there's a pock-marked man in a cardigan wailing, 'I am twenty nations' and shaking his fake Swiss Army knife at a brood of saplings whisking in the mist.

*

Ah, a fresh fall of snow, I note with approval, coming out into the freezing night to head back to the studio. But it's just old snow the keen wind has shifted and set down on the gritted road. No, my fatted, lovesunk heart insists, it's New Snow. And who am I to argue?

*

I am wading through the chapters of *My Life with Elk*: two hairy sisters charge me as I lock up the Valentine, making my heart thud; as we walk towards the smelly springs, a bruiser stag stares me down and eyes the tomboy Jo; a whole troupe surrounds the studio and I claim kin, dropping to all fours to join them; late one night, a she-elk brushes the pine branches like a lady novelist skimming through the frock racks in a fancy store.

*

The song 'Waiting for the Miracle' lifts my head from a book in welcome recognition, as if it doesn't matter that my copy of it is on a cassette, in my parents' attic, thousands of miles away, and the case written out in too-neat handwriting by a girl I lost years ago to Jesus Christ.

*

Lacking the benefit of fruit machines, late night true crime or the chance of dozing over love memories on the 38 bus, I find myself asking what matters more – Truth or New Experience? To all-comers, I explain New Experience, of course, but once the porch door here is locked, I understand that it may involve Brussels sprouts, kissing a man with a beard, or the six years darg it would take me to play that grand piano behind me which looks every day more like a black bull closing in to gore.

Cover Versions

The two authenticated skulls of Cromwell:
one explained as his childhood skull.

Twenty line-ups of The Drifters crooning
to OAPs in shabby, beachside ballrooms.

Three hundred thousand splinters of The True Cross.
You, Roddy, somewhere in the morning.

On the Cusp of Virgo and Libra

Because the wheel fell off the wall and since
the bullmoth butted me and left
a musky stain, the nine of us
on milking stools and not one life
untouched, unspiked by bitterness,
and since the sluice had bowed
and gutted to a trickle and the curtilage

was singed by late high summer,
the sprinklers' coils kinked and creased,
the heron having spooled the pond
and borrowed up a mottled koi,
night air's maneater tang did not prevent
the spats and clashes, hard embraces
in the cellar, gentle weeping not far off,

a full glass fired across the courtyard
and because the chimney kindled
and seeing that the wine was corked
and since the sweat dropped off us all,
hounds keened in the wood nearby
and the casserole was salty
as we ate from paper plates;

because the news of war is constant
and the good books dry of succour,
9 *Down* unsolved in the crossword,
yet since the scales are bound to balance
and neither pan will dip for long and we
were aimed at nowhere, less than wretched,
so it was we knew that they had prospered.

Specific Hunger

It's not enough to say a briny air
coasts off the gorge, that my downstairs neighbour
is basting a crisp-coated broiler,
that garlic and cardamom ghost on my hands
from the weekend's wondrous korma –

at times the craving is narrowed down,
shaved to a pill, hunted across fields to a den
where it surrenders and reveals itself
as chicken in soy sauce from that takeaway
long since demolished; the unlikely delicacy

of tinned risotto bubbled in its can;
sweet deep-fried sausages from a chip shop
on the back roads of Fife circa '71;
My eyes gloom up with lust, my mouth is rife,
the belly keening. The best of us mourn the loss

of such salt tongue blessings, part savour
and part pity, which we will not taste again:
musky pakora sauce subliming on my wrists
as I drifted home across The Meadows;
a lentil soup so true I knelt and wept.

Perfumes of Scotland

– **Katabella** running shoeless up the snow-chilled burn – **Trinquet** behind the ears of the minister's wife as she trowels the pebbly earth beneath the buddleia – **Scrufan** at midday, breathe in the scent of brickfields stumped along the disused branch line – **Gussie** a scarlet kiss by the dry dock **Whishie** the wildcat marking the way-lanes of his province – **Bomacie** the night filling and fusing as we lie dizzy on the dike with a bottle, a sputter of static – **Dunino** pine-sap, coot-call, roe-trail – **Truelins** the night tide rooting through banks of shells – **Ferintosh** treacle baccy smoke betraying the beater drawn into the shady abature – **Wildrif** danced out, half-dressed and gasping – **Immer** for widows only, worn as far afield as Meg's Craig, Latheronwheel and Damnaglaur – **Smitch** a petrol spill in a car park at the back of the rink – **Floshan** fresh dew on the fifteenth green, the flag charmed by the first of the breeze – **Aiverin** moss on a picture book thrown in the stank – **Okraquoy** sweetroot breaching the breakwater, muscling through cracks in the pier – **Merrigle** a tenement tap left on an hour till the water is gospel cold –

Conspiracy Sketch

Here. But not now.

LORRIE MOORE, 'Like Life'

Skimming up the lade in dew-soaked clothes,
he daydreams you back once more, lean-clad
once more and poised there on the stairhead,
hands knitted at your nape, arms angel's wings.

At the wood's brink, he stares as havoc-birds
swarm above the stacks; the hanging gate
lours above the mill-stream. Should anyone
enter that room where you had lain together,

night might tumble quick, the air would curdle
with dripping nixes, quaking polts, the howling
of the black shuck. Dark presses would rumble
in canyon hangars. News will reach the world.

True Believers

Nothing goes clear. Did Jesus smoke, or Caesar?
Does black light settle on the waterside
or does the water procure the black light
wholesale, from the reasonable sky?

Should I believe in sortilege, in sidelong
advances? I am thinking that the gentle come
to cling together and yes, that's a thick flag
of ice on the Red River, a quicksand season,

you can't force luck on the only road. I am thinking
of how the gentle come to cling together,
of our two options, sweet girl, as smoke settles
along night paths. Now is one. Or Never.

Miss America

He never thought it would be you.

It was *a long hour*'s drive from Grand Forks back to Fargo
and a high moon, one day shy of full, loitered
in prairie sky above the cloister barns, the snoozing hawks,
the tearaway romance of us;
     the glowing horizon was an age-wide hoop
which shifted in inches, sure to keep us
drifting as its centre point;
     I noticed all this in the moments I transferred my gaze
from the real scenery – your sleepy, lovely eyes

framed in the rear-view, switching from the long
black road behind, to the one good road ahead.
Spotless through intrigue, our pairing time
was short, a storm game, our team-mates shocked
(the *Girlfriend Shop* I'd sworn to walk on past took stock).
     On Midwestern Thursdays,
the stockyards burn the blood of pigs, on Sundays
the blood of the lamb redeems.
     Stand high, America!

When *Blood on the Tracks* ran twice, although 'Idiot Wind'
     never sounded as sweet,
I wanted *Miss America*, to hear Mary Margaret singing
     'Help Me Lift You Up' knowing
that 'You Will Be Loved Again' would follow at the end,
the disc spinning down in silence, the dark journey done
and you would draw into the driveway, wild for holding,
the warmth you sought out on the cold edge of me
roaring on the last of five true nights.

One Acre Yard

(Fargo, North Dakota)

April – we have missed the thaw by days;
the yard rolls pale in its narrow palette
of oatmeals and ochre; only the spruce
busks its darkness down each limit.

All that has fallen these months
now gains at last the effortless glory
of standstill, dropped through the slush
those last redemptive inches; the story

twisting in its final paragraphs, debris settling:
these beer tins, deer scat, thrawn branks
of a long-rooted plum tree; a frozen raven
who has wintered here on his black back

welcomes the sun and softens, unzips
his coat to show his bones and basks
as warmth infects the air; the terrier inspects
her tenth season of this snow-stung grass.

And us. We walk the acre arm in arm,
still melting from our shyness, to the river
freshened and shirring at its banks, all harm
on ice and the worst of winters over.

from

THE BUBBLE BRIDE

(2003)

Sang o' the Kittock's Loddie

Gin a nicht lik this wad aince mair fin me –
whan horrit, skeely-pussit birks
glaumin an ruskin in the mirk
gan suddent douce an a warm saut-wund quhyds
whiles, wi a soond lik a kirkfu o clareschaws,
the souch daffs the beuchs whaur lang-luggit houlets
deuk on their spakes, teetin gin a shear moose
wad chance throu the windlestrae.

Gin a byspale nicht lik thon wad fin me –
whan the brockie snavils and creachles on his clump
an, shoosh, yon's the yaup o a bizzart wi wan ee
steek tae the bizzin warld,
the tither in a dwaum o a thoosand skelterin rattons;
gentie does tipper throu the flush, bawties
coorie in clappards, the linn skills ontae the syver
an syne the blackfuit's sleekit wark is duin.

Gin ah micht teal yon teeger tae me:
ma teeniebash an fliskmahoy, ma romp
slinkin doon the brae intil the den at trysted-oor:
the twa ae's fu tae the thrapples, no wi wheef
or swat bit in a swander, hairts trouncin,
temerare, an by, fidder an het aneath me,
the kittock cheetin hinnie lees
an the hale rairin nicht yit tae come!

TRANSLATION: *Song of the Minx's Swain*

If only a night like this would find me again – when horrible, scaly-faced birches, snatching and scratching in the darkness, turn suddenly calm and a warm salt wind blows gently while, with a sound like a church full of harps, the breeze moves the branches where long-eared owls bob on their perches, watching in case a shrew should chance through the withered grass.

If only a wondrous night like that one would find me – when the badger snuffles and coughs huskily on his heap and, hush, that's the faint cry of a buzzard with one eye shut to the bustling world, the other in a dream of a thousand scuttling rats; elegant does tiptoe through the marshy surface, rabbits snuggle in burrows, the waterfall spills onto the field drain and then the go-between's cunning work is done.

If only I might entice that tigress to me: my young flirt and frivolous girl, my jade sneaking down the slope into the dell at the meeting-hour: the two of us full to the throats, not with liquor or beer but in a swoon, hearts rushing, reckless and, soon, excited and hot beneath me, the minx telling sweet lies and the whole roaring night still to come!

A Saltire

Two churnfuls of first milk flushed
across a farmland, night-time sky,
the cross flag juts and fluthers
over a St Andrews bay,
unworked by jibs and rudders,
but undone by small, hard waves, its sheen
mingles, one moment skirting-board grey,
the next the tones of a chic silk stole.

Here, where a saint's bones still knock
in the broth, in current-chiselled troughs
ten fathoms down, where last squibs
of fluorine sea-light
dance off dark hulks of rock,
igniting the shells of sculling shrimps,
kicking their frills from relic to relic,
rolling in a thousand acre feet of swell;

humerus, canine, patella brought to us
at *the north-west ends of the earth*
by Regulus, mad dreaming monk
or money maker,
shipwrecked sailor shivering in his cave,
shaking the salt spray from his hair
and weeping for a handful of bleached,
Greek fingers the bay still crosses for luck.

Hotel Showers of the World

Before you step into the mist and spray
be sure that water is plentiful nearby:
you could look across the great, grey Bay
from Manila's Pan Pacific; the walk-in
was bigger than back rooms I've lived in –
hot rain pummelled my awkward bones,
volcanic flush direct from Pinatubo.
At The Warder's Inn in Lewes, a worn rose
sent down a rope of warm water, catching
on my nape, a gift from the hanging judges
at the local assizes, who once hoisted cads
into their nooses while the Ouse
rounded a slack corner.
                  Up in Stockholm,
the Berns had one neat hole in the ceiling,
another in the cambered floor
and a swing-out panel, enough of a door
as you'd need; boats frothed snug quays
a stroll away; the cathedral bell slammed.
At The St Andrews Bay, I crank
the overdrive and, miles away, unseen,
mallards will bob distractedly
as the reservoir surrenders a half inch
to leave me this pink, this clean.

The Kitchens: A Guided Tour

That's not a pneumatic drill but a giant's wazzer
for puréeing soup. Cast an eye on this identity parade
of carboys filled with dressings – caraway, juniper,
mustard and cumin seed. Cooks waltz in and out.
A coldchest, winking between three and four degrees,
is temporary home to French smoked chickens,
Danish salamis, sliced rolled Wurst, finest pancetta,

a fat hand of heat-sealed chorizos. There are no muses
for the stockman's art, for the whisker's knack
and the slicer's craft, the guile you need with pastry.
That's a sink deep-filled with chilling cos; coffers
marked *glass cloths* or *linen only*; tubs of 'TASKI profi'
and 'Suma shine' lie ready. A primed supply
of toast racks, ramekins, cakestands and the eggcups

show their little faces below the WANTED shots
of waiters-of-the-month. Here's the infernal machine
where dirty strainers, streaky cleavers, oily woks
and steamy colanders go to get clean. *Hot – don't touch!*
Dinner plates are sent to their doom in the Comenda
and set back fresh in stacks of pearl, bubblegum
and bottle green; we want our glasses 'all to polished'

and there in a corner, a breakage tray like Kim's game
gone wrong. Planning to serve Glayva and tablet?
Here's a 'how to' demo photo. A regiment of milk jugs
is ready to advance. 'FIND OUT – FIND OUT EVERYTHING'
A Crypto Peerless, on its dinner-hour, waits to knead
whatever you need to knead. We are cosmopolitans –
Brazilian figs, Dutch courgette fleurs, Canary toms,

our baby fennel is Pyrenean. Our oatmeal is pinhead
stoneground Scotch – seeing as it's you. Remember,
we *read the guests, anticipate their needs!*
And we anticipate their tongues, we anticipate crumbs,
we anticipate sighs as they un-notch their belts
and sit back, sighs of satisfaction rising in the atrium,
the last mouthful of merlot still to be savoured.

On the Boat-slope

Pinned upon the harbour head,
I found a scribbled note which said,
*'She who has beauty is better dead
than tangling with the boys.'*

The young ones walked the pier and back
in scarlet gowns and Sunday tack
except for one dressed down in black
who sat in sulken poise

upon the boat-slope listlessly
and moaned for one more true than me.
The grim and bubbling of the sea
rose all above the noise.

The Bubble Bride

(in the hydrotherapy bath, The St Andrews Bay Hotel)

As I sink in, she taunts me and I purl and rollick,
my knuckles splaying; my legs are pilloried
to keep me in my place; her ways are wiles,
so much going on beneath her surface
and when she lets off steam, her scents are citrus,
carrots, coconut and pine. My blood chicanes,
raises its game, and says *okay*. She bids me sweat
and grabs me by the shoulders, birling me,
lambada, tango, waltz in triple triple time, a Bach
cantata capers up and someone chants in Basque,
my spine's a glockenspiel; she pushes me
into a crowd with a place-to-be and fast,
foaming, swirling me now while squibs leap up
and puddles puff and pop-guns volley off.
Her fingers tingle soles and calves, my sides
are split with tickles, swollen muscles
soothed and scapulae placated, my bride-
to-be makes me a fizzcake fusing in the water,
her ration, her ruddy Romeo, her helping:
a suddy and sizzling Szechuan platter, full,
willing and fuelling the bathsides with my breath,
my heart thudding and scudding in the surge,
her spray played at my nape, I call, *I will. I will!*
And from the spa, the bridesmaid in her white uniform
slips in to check the job is done and, in the gloam,
a vapour trousseau, a cumulus of sultry weather
roils wet and warm around the treatment room.
I lie here, the muttering groom, a lulling tide
of semi-sleep shifting in me and the bubble bride
parading up and down my back forever.

Spent

On the map of want, I'm in the wood-light
at Brigton, skirring the fallen egg-shells
beneath my boot at the head of the track
or skithering on a brace of birch logs, braving
the gape of the gulley which flaunts
ice water laced with empty sulphate sacks
and cartridges, runs past the Anderson shelter
where lies what might have then been mine:
the soiled clothes and billy-can, the torn-at pages
of dreaming matter; spent time; a thorn on a thorn
on a thorn; the bings of chaff and leaf-litter
through which I wade to the woods' end
where ten fields fill my eye
each billowing and calling to me, *I'm the one.*

Lateral Vertigo

As soon as you let the lift close
at your back, then you will sense
the Good Book *for the use*
of successive users; the vanity kit:
a tile-slide puzzle you will not solve;
the pan-national vocabulary
of toiletries:
                    now hear the pressure
drop in decibels, in the op art corridor
a full four bowling alleys long,
carpeted to minimise your footfalls;
this wind tunnel where Icarus
had slipped, one foot from the sea;
where snoring trains pass at once
on both sides of the platform;
a long lateral where housemaids
and concierges drift, to catch us
should we chance too close to land.

Overheard in a Scottish Larder

Wi ma lug tae the freezin door o the larder,
I cuid hear twa voices bickerin within:
wan cries, Scotch pies, bridies an butteries.
The ither says, canon o Perthshire lamb.
The first says, truckles o hramsa an crowdie,
the ither, slabs of caboc, morven an dunlop.
Wan suggests a darn of fresh Tay-caught slamon.
The ither plumps fir a tian of sweet partan crab.

Wan screams fir black bun an petticoat tails,
the ither fir girdle scones, teabreads an bannocks.
Wan declares Drambuie cream-topped cranachan.
The ither unwraps tablet an toffee wi a coo on it.
Wan says, surely, rumbledethumps an stovies!
The ither's for bashed tatties, sybies an clapshot.
Ah'm thirsty fir Irn Bru an Red Kola, says wan.
Ah'm drier fir Deuchars an Laphroaig, goes the ither.

When wan langs fir soor plooms an Edinburgh rock,
the ither sickens fir Snowballs and Caramel Logs.
Shout aye tae inginy skirlie and mealie puddin!
Naw, taste some clootie dumplin and white puddin!
Try compote on your porridge, says the first.
Tak saut and a grummle wi yer porridge, says th'ither.
Says wan, ah'll be roastin venison the day.
Says the next, ah'm tea-smokin doos the day.

Rasps straicht fae the Carse of Gowrie, cries ane.
Rain-fed brambles fae Fife hedgerows, says the ither.
The first goes, dinnae let on what a haggis is,
the ither goes, *nivver* let on what a haggis is.
A platefu' o Scotch broth or Royal Game, mibbe?
Naw, a dish o cullen skink or cock-a-leekie!
Says wan, it'll crawl roond yer hairt lik a hairy worm.
Eat up, yer at yer blind auntie's, cries the ither.

Lumsden Hotel

The kilted porter shook my hand in welcome,
drained it of blood and gave me back my luggage.
I signed the register in my own name
for the first time in my life of low celebrity.
In the lounge bar, there were pictures by Margarita
but no sign of margaritas by the pitcher.
All night, the couple in the next-door room
failed noisily to make love even once.
The signature tune of the air conditioning
was a surefire B-side for any one-hit-wonder.
Weary, I ordered up the late night menu
from room service, but sleep wasn't on it
so, after an hour of mentally undressing myself,
I donned the pyjamas with the killer bee motif
and there on the bed I wrote a dozen
identical postcards to friends I'd forgotten.
No doubt to keep the cold tap company,
the hot tap had opted to be a cold tap too.
Funnel-web spiders wove their lazy way
toward each other across the scarlet ceiling
and when I solved the riddle of the shower,
no blood came gushing, but no water either.
By the bed, a Gideon Bible in Esperanto
and a phone-book listing Lumsdens of the world;
in the mini-bar, flat Vimto and a half-pint
of someone else's mother's milk, turned to fur.
The TV had one channel, showing highlights
from my worst performances in every sphere.
At three, in the courtyard, a chambermaid choir
sang a barbershop version of 'I Will Survive'.
The only time I dared to close my eyes,
dervishes under the bed began to talk dirty.
When I left at nine and settled my check,
they told me clearly *Don't come back.*

Little Fife

(after Kathleen Ossip)

Mind and get in behind that gritter. The Romans did *sut*
make it this far North! Stewing juniper pickles the wind.
I'm fair puggled after going the messages. I'm told Robinson
Crusoe was born in a but'n'ben down by the shore. *Jings!*

The guide-book says the chippy has changed hands
in Newburgh. There's no white puddin. The town no longer
even smells of lino. A golden eagle's been spotted moping
out by Hazelton Walls and a puma sniffing the mean streets

of Methil. Mary Queen of Scots lifted her skirts here. *Shoosh!*
It was just the golf-ball sized hailstones on the windscreen
woke you. Wee fuds skoosh into the wood's edge. *Sorry,*
the onion bridies are done, will half a mince round

do you? It's half day in Windygates so away and comb
monkeys. Your first cairn is an occasion, I grant you, but
by the fifth, you're *like that. How huge is that bing?*
Hang on, we're getting near Kilconquhar where the Cooncil

are building Little Fife, the whole Kingdom in miniature.
Is that a haar or is it just me? Get that! *A hitcher wi' a sign*
saying DUNDEE. The Singing Kettle going techno is jist
deep down tragic. *As I've said before, Vettriano is so much more*

than a MacHopper. Ye've got tae give a limpet a right good kick.
Scotrail welcomes you to Leuchars station. *I used to love*
the waltzer like, but these days I'm that gruey. Sunny spells are
promised for the evening. *I hate hats but I'll hae tae hae a hat.*

Evidence of Owls

Unthinkable jewels,
these pellets laced with a trinkum of mouse-spines
and the black jeel eyes of creeping things.

One wing feather,
a blade of cream, tan, honey, amber, ochre,
flutters on the turf wall of a bunker.

A starter's car arrives,
its headlights flooding two infernal eyes
wheedling the clubhouse and the whins.

Conclusive evidence –
a crescent of static which quick wings
have left behind still seethes and cozens:

a gap in the dawn air over Kittock's Den.

from

RODDY LUMSDEN IS DEAD

(2001)

Forget good deeds and great works, forget theorems and inventions. We ought to judge a man by how many women weep at his funeral.

JOSEPH TOURNEFORT

When combined with guilt, depersonalisation and de-realisation may be ominous symptoms because they enable the patient to take cold-blooded steps to destroy himself without normal awareness of the significance and consequences of what he does.

The Oxford Companion to the Mind

My Pain

...one begins, ungratefully, to long for the contrasting tone of
some honest, unironic misery, confident that when it arrives
Roddy Lumsden will have the technical resources to handle it.
NEIL POWELL, *TLS*

I'm trying to string together three words
which I hate more than I hate myself:
gobsmacked, hubby and...when I realise
that words no longer count for much at all.

And that's me back down, head on the floor.
It's like Cathal Coughlan goes in his song:
I don't think I'll rise again
till I've seen how low I can go.

It's like what my ancestor told me in a dream:
You'll be a sponge for the pain of others.
It's like what I told the lassie from the local paper:
I do not suffer for my art, I just suffer.

And face it, while we're at it, it's like
what curly Shona said that night at Graffiti
when all the gang were gathered for the show:
how she reckoned I would be the first to die,

or the time I slipped back from the bogs in Bo's
to hear my best friend tell a stranger girl
who'd been sweet in my company, *mind how you go*
with Roddy, he's damaged goods, you know.

My Death

A woman's silver shoe remains sole-up
beneath a broken chair. A china cup

with half an inch of something sour and green.
A thin, white line divides the TV screen.

Bouts of thunder shift the world all day.
A sweet voice says, *hold tight, it's time to pay.*

Millions quietly talk of their diseases.
The black-hubbed wind does as it pleases.

My Funeral

Wrapped in *The Scotsman*,
the family hamster

in a Saxone shoe box
four feet under;

a suburban witch digging
in the mid of the winter

with a string-tied parcel
whose shape is familiar;

a dead-weight coffin
dropped into a merchant sea.

Will I bury my mother?
Will my mother bury me?

My Allegory

Mad as honey, jinking in and out of traffic
where Manor Road and Stamford Hill meet up,
a boy holds in front of him a broken slab
of mirror, walking blind while staring back.

It's a sure-fire metaphor for *something*, the very image
you'd spend a fortnight gasping for – an allegory
for the collapse of a community which once
left doors unlocked and meat pies cooling on sills.

Perhaps. Or for the extinction of elaborate species,
the wayward progress of genetic engineering,
for the hotbed introspection of the artist,
for saints, fizzled to ciphers, who left us praying.

Or an allegory for the thoughts which swell my head
when you hold me in the lane behind the sweet shop.
That is, if metaphors for thoughts are still allowed
on this plundered and squandered nosebag of a planet.

My Early Years

These last days in the back room at Manor Road
are plied with phantom scents: yesterday,
the air sharpened with the tang of sweet sherbet –
the stuff which was decanted, from a bottle
filled with gaudy drifts, into white paper pokes.
Today, it was the smell of pink bubble gum:
of Bubbly say, or sickly Bazooka Joe.
The main thing is, though others may know better,
I remember my boyhood as a happy time,
a silver time before the jolt of knowledge,
the shocks of ECT, the shock of love.
Look, there's Margaret, my childhood sweetheart
waving at me across two hedges. And here's
my best sand castle tilting its little flag at the tide.

My Hormones

Does it begin with the still-warm waltzer seat
where fairground scientists detect
my Kirlian aura, a wraith wisp of candy-floss
and the outro to 'Ashes to Ashes'
by now only audible to a pack of dogs

who would blench and bay at the presence
of the White Lady pacing through the walls
of the ruined cathedral and would rather be
the Baron's harriers trailing through Tentsmuir,
bowling down that me-shaped abature?

Or is it in the moss and raindrop endocrinology
of the ninth hole of the East Bents putting green
which sits above the North Sea's stately nausea
as it washes through the boat-stones of the pier
where students parade in scarlet gowns:

these blunt blokes set on degrees in geography
and horsy girls from Roedean and Cheltenham
with their slang beauty, who, reaching the end,
can make the walk back, or jump on in? We poets
should keep our damned hands off each other.

My Water

The ox-bow lake where every creature
is the final generation of its species.
The river bottom where the proving's done.
The dish-slops where the mince-grease sails,
blown by the whore's-blench of my breath.
The wishing well run dry. A mill wheel
rusted to whimsy. Prisms in the sluice.
The bath gone cold before you're into it.
There's aye some water whaur the stirkie drouns.
Atlantic meets Pacific. Streams of piss.
The days I wasted by the Maiden Rock
building dams where cold, cold water
tripped down from the farmer's fields,
to stop my life becoming all it is.

My National Stigma

One winter's night in the Princess Louise,
when a brace of shaggy moths flew up
from the depths of my tartan wallet,
the Londoners said they felt ready at last
to ask me The Scottish Questions:
inevitable ones about the kilt, the work ethic,
the repression thing, our fabled gallon bellies.
And no, it wasn't true that we were mean –
hadn't I just stood a round of halves? –
that was just the silver-shy Aberdonians
and to them, just the Kittybrewster folk,
and to the folks of Kittybrewster, just Nan
and Jim Buchan in their bungalow, tugging
a stray penny between them, inventing wire.

My Limbo

It doesn't take the full-wind sickness,
just the mere, the constant threat of it,
just the salt trace, its faint knocking
to bring the spirits of chance and chaos
into this house – they stand in doorways:
quaint, foul allies, swivelling their ghost hips,
tugging at their gowns of transparency
and mischief. They buzz me with lust,
and I'm undone.
     Remember these: the Cupid
who ducked up from behind a wall and aimed
an arrow, one evening on Broughton Street;
whatever grabbed my shoulder at Earlshall;
a sound of heavy boxes pushed up and down
the empty hallway; the past is the self's ghoul.
What is it, Roddy, you know you've blocked out?
What left your brain so empty that it gushed full
with circus music and the safe bet of trivia?
Here I am swinging on the fence of fences, in limbo,
where the other world loves to try my pragmatism
and it's I who have invited them, summoned
by this self-indulgent ouija.
     But what is it
that folds my clothes as I sleep and leaves them
on the edge of the bed? Who hides my slippers,
re-hangs the paintings? *Déjà vu.* Did a minor
goddess filch me in Manila and follow me home,
prone, as they are, to easy-led mortal men.
And I'm easy, easy. So, come now, teach me
to believe in the soul. Hurt me with the truth. Press
me back down on this cheap, wine-coloured carpet;
let me know for once and for all how fucked I am.

My Face Not Fitting

One night, way back in the Royal Oak,
two stranger girls were asked to guess
what it was I did for a living
or what it looked like I might do
for a living of sorts. And by and by
they came up with computer operator
and lawnmower repair man.
So it is I am among the number
of the Poets Who Do Not Look Like Poets:
you-know-who – the dominatrix in civvies;
Dreamgirl, with her county-set hostess looks
and that voice which could frenzy a stallion
and so-and-so with his ba'-heid, so
Irish looking that you expect to find him
untacking waffles of mud from boots
in the Shamrock Rovers dressing room
or topping and tailing turnips on Moore Street.

My Half-life

I was aware of me myself in the exact middle of a living story,
and my body was my adventure and my name.
DYLAN THOMAS, The Peaches

...but it was the phrase 'literally a goddess'
which took my ear, with its double-take logic,
its layers of fabulous imprecision, its position

just around the next bend in a moral maze –
how it made me realise my life is now half over,
bringing as it did pearls of memory: that first

and only time I undressed Cerys
or Becky on the tennis lawn at Earlshall
rehearsing that speech from *Lovers: Winners.*

My Sex Life

Come on everybody. Especially you girls.
Each day I think of something about dying.
                    DENISE RILEY, Shantung

When those things happen
you thought would never happen
and they happen gently
on sweet-smelling beds in back rooms;

when you find a mouth
which completes the machine of yours –
two halves of a split penny reunited;
when you unbutton a body so perfect

and rounded it dips into the abstract;
when two girls invite you to cancel
the bed-space between them
and one is gun-metal

and the other cherry red;
if you find you were wrong
in thinking your next sighting
of a naked teenager would be

an embarrassing confrontation
with a grown-up daughter;
when such things occur,
there is something pulls us upwards,

farther than the hormonal rockets,
and that thing is the state of grace
from which, on my brief pyre of optimism,
I believe I will never recover.

My Ascent

When dawn broke, I cast a little stone
into the mist ahead. Back came a rock.

I put my plans together, sharpened sticks
and flipped them through the fog. By nine o'clock,

I'd done the battle-axe, a steel harpoon
and by elevenses, the Gatling gun.

By four, I'd built a ship and reached the moon.

My Descent

On a day like this, a palm placed
face down on the scalp
is enough to soften my skull.

One finger rested on the throat
will buckle the jaw
and I will speak no more.

Your hand pressed at my belly
drains my insides
of knowledge and order.

All this by way of healing me.
I must have faith in you,
for it's a long and wild way home.

I will feel my feathers fall,
my hard scales slough.
We'll crawl together to the sea.

My Superstition

The toreador insect, the size and colour
of a brazil nut (unshelled) which I brought
all the way from Negros Occidental,
stowed away in my outsize hold-all,
now finds its way along the skirting-board
and begins to ascend the bookcase.
By way of entomancy, we will tell
what my life will make of me, but while
it climbs, there's time enough to roll-call
my superstitions: all those envelopes
I kissed for luck; the scissors I make
of my fingers to snip the invisible ropes
round my waist when I turn full circle;
the years of obsession with the number four.
The bug parades past Burnside, Copus,
bypasses *Brewer's*, *Chambers*, *Nil Nil*,
not yet noticing the volume on the floor
inside which it is fated to crawl and die
between the lines of the last paragraph
which describe how my childless ancestor
lay down, fixing to die, on a distant island,
his ear to the hard sand not yet hearing
the wet footfalls of the woman, peeling
and unpeeling through the shallows,
spoiling the silence of the moonlit cove.

My Luck

They say I'm the head of a brutalist school
just because I've always known my place
and taken my chances. The floor is strewn
with grapes and gooseberries where Fortune
has slipped and spilled the Cornucopia,
now just a filthy goat's horn hollowed out.
She lies concussed, her skirt about her thighs,
twitching the Rudder this way and that.

My Reflection

A man dies and leaves a name; the tiger dies and leaves a skin.
CHINESE PROVERB

Late-night and bearded, framed in a mirror
as make-believe Rouault judge, white-faced and counting
his sins and his blessings – although I have neither –

I call myself sufferer, suitor, survivor,
repeating each, eitherwise deeming and doubting,
and switch between Budweiser, Silk Cut and cider.

The tiger feels no need to call himself Tiger.
He spends the night brassily whoring and hunting
and sees himself briefly at dawn in the river.

He paws at his rival, who ripples to nothing.

My Sickness

A taint in the blood of my ancestry
(gracious, field-snug Chalmers blood),
a blind bend in the brain's maze
means that one of us is taken
from the back lines of the herd
from time to time.
                        Aunt Belle
was dragged down in the shallows of old age,
unexpected. She sank fast and succumbed
before my first sickness had its full thirst.
In a late, lucid hour, she made acceptance:
there's nothing they can do for me now,
but Roddy must be saved.
                                I wasn't yet
inside the mouth of the whale
but I was fathoms under and couldn't hear
them screaming for me up above
and the bad salt taste of it is in me still.

My Performance

Hélène Cixous, paralysed, blinks
and blinks through borrowed time
and the alphabet of her life story.

Billy Idol, raven-haired and stocky
and preening at a tinny mic,
bawling out 'I'm Mandy, Fly Me'.

Jenny Saville chewing on a brush,
directing a spindly chorus line of fey
Elite girls, teetering on racer bikes.

And here's me discovering the price
and the cost of my performance piece:
Roddy Lumsden – Char Siu Boy.

80

My Realm of the Senses

the liquoricy stink of badger dirt
a mouthful of pig's thinkers, chilled and raw
the cookie-dough complexion of the heart
that you need to be touched just there just so
the spitting sound of burning pigeon-wings
I know I know I shouldn't know such things.

My Plea

Please once, at last, to be desired
for what I am not who I am.
To be loved for my stash of fire
and not my store of wonder.
I want love to be hollow, sham;
I long to be held under.

My Meeting with the Goddess

You remember how, in the story,
the academic is shopping for socks
in a mall in Manila when the goddess
appears in the form of a shop assistant
who touches his beloved face and disappears.
My goddess decides to show herself
at a workshop in a sleepy Highland town.

She has chosen a champion disguise –
a restless German redhead, at least my age,
in a cardigan sewn with beads of rain
which shine there all weekend and never dry.
There's a new identity she's been devising
ever since she followed me back here
from the dark, sugar streets of Bacolod:

she's sweet but complicated, divorced,
a lapsed romantic wearing a cynic's hat,
with a wheat-free diet and six years
in the Findhorn Foundation behind her
(a nice cryptotheological touch that)
and a bachelorette pad over in Avoch
where she secretly whips up pans of *adobo*.

We escape to the firth-front to wolf
great platters of breaded seafood and salad,
to wrestle with tartare sauce sachets; our pasts
are shadowy, because she's a goddess
and because ECT wiped half of mine.
I recall something about a putting green;
she talks of a brief marriage in Switzerland.

I try her with *Unterhaltungsmöglichkeiten*
and *Selbstbedienungslebensmittelgeschäft*
and she laughs politely *(bahala na!)*,
batting them back with a Graf forehand.
Highland dogs cruise the streets; for once
I do not take the chance they afford
to move in close. I should have embraced

my goddess, should have held her hand
if only to feel it disappear in mine,
to see her shrink away, casting me adrift
in the back streets of a Black Isle town.
And weeks later, flying down to Galway
there she'll be again beside me: her thighs
broader and longer, the cute, tippy-toe walk

that screamed *Not German* gone, her nose
in a trashy Scottish novel (another nice touch),
but it *will* be her, biddable and tolerant her,
willing to deliver my baby-face, girl to girl
and town to town, in my time of sluttery.
For now, I leave her, dram in hand, at the bar,
talking to some local worthy, her accent

shifting from Negros to Bayern to Easter Ross
and tomorrow I will wake in the Japanese annexe:
my pomegranate mouth, my yak flank hair,
the skin of my back busy with mill-sweat,
feet beeling and dinging like buck-rabbits
and a dispirited girl will play a Chopin Nocturne
over and over, through in the sunlit lounge

as if someone had written a script.
Sorry: as if someone *hadn't* written a script.

My Prayer

For all the fools in loveless marriages,
for all the wretches stuck in dullard jobs,
for those in peril in the sea of faces
or stranded in the gyms or jails or pubs.

For all those under mental anaesthetic,
and those who're wrestling with the other self,
for all the dreamers starving in an attic,
and poor souls held at ransom by their health.

For those who live their lives in constant darkness,
for those who sold out years ago, please may
the emotional tourist in each one of us
cast anchor in a sun-spoilt bay.

My Future

I think I know now what will happen:
Nature, after abhorring the vacuum,
will turn to me,
will stretch my body on a frame of urges –
the bachelor wild at the foot of the bride.

My Solitude

Though we would wish to keep them with us,
we may need the beautiful to be with each other,
may feel it right and proper, in just the way
we cannot stop ourselves from finishing
a drawing of a face without the eyes.

Yesterday on the tube up to Chalk Farm,
to my left, there was a gorgeous woman
sitting with a chump and to my right
a square-cut guy with a kind face, so why
was he with that gawky puppet of a girl?

Some bilk; some take the wrong fork in the road,
but *fitness is the keystone of survival*.
And so I understand my solitude
and how this poem begins with my eavesdropping
a prediction of my early death

among my extended family of Edinburgh friends –
now sainted or broken or plain unchanged –
and ends here on Manor Road
by way of love songs, cognac and phantoms.
A few months single. Amicable. Mutual.

And lately, I find my affairs with women
freshly complex, keenly confusing –
the ex-loves, the half-loves, crushes, obsessions –
and I think of that old crowd, how I miss them,
looking out on the tracks here in cold North London.

Does it read like a draft for a suicide note?
For it's not that, never – not with the protection
of the other self (though *that* rogue might do it).
No, I've a coldness: a cool – not a cruel – streak,
the film star's full camouflage wardrobe, a soundtrack.

Here's a thumbed copy of *The Year's Afternoon*
by Douglas Dunn in the pocket of my car-coat.
Poor Douglas, out in his garden at Dairsie,
rocked dizzy by love in a way that I envy –
strangely – I, who must look through a glass

not darkly, but always, who can only focus
on one thing at one time with any fullness,
for whom grieving is just a vague stirring,
slipping as I do into my sickness
when danger starts up its solemn knocking.

And, sorry, I never do see it coming.
These days I find myself checking the window
of The Daniel Defoe and I know I am looking
for that girl – plump, fair-haired and twenty –
who sits there alone, composing poetry.

And what would it be like? Honest and plucky,
I reckon, wearing its flaws like hackles
on a cockerel and that is just as it should be.
Make no apology for your apology.
Quite soon in the script, that's what I say to her.

My Life

The fig was full of worms.
The joke was on me.
The joke went over my head.
I made myself hollow for others.
I took delight in the sight of a trap.
I learned to lie with grace.
I tried to hide horned animals in a sack.
I ate the food and then the food ate me.
And when at last I danced the music stopped.
The cream was skimmed too soon.
My wings and tail were plucked.
My mouth was primed with mud.
My larynx was a shrine.
I left the room to talk about the others.
The thorn in time extracts the thorn.
My years were two of yours.
No bird was of my feather.
I was blait and toom and fykesome.
The rice just wouldn't fluff.
I never lived it up
and never lived it down.
The fish was full of bones.
The skunk curled on my lap.
I was torn in the bush of ghosts.
The point was not worth proving:
the proof was in the pudding
in the form of a split penny.
The jellyfish was in my mouth.
The landslide happened in my mouth.
I pressed and pressed the button
but Truth wouldn't happen.
Time wasted me and I wasted time,
like the night lost in the wynds
and back lanes, searching for a strut
that will take my weight when the time is right.

My Pennyworth

So many are out there
saying the moon is beautiful
but not placing their hands
on the soft skin of its neck.
Know that, in your silence,
you have a sky in which
any hand might touch you.

My Spring
(after March)

As some malingerer, a long time sick,
strives to force his raw-boned, bedsore body
up, one sunburst morning, muscles weak
and ribs ill-ricked, then so it is with Roddy
who wrestles with the memory of love
and who, despite his rumoured bag of brains,
can't pin the bastard, since no brawn remains
after the barb-strung malady of love.

BUT SWEET

The Consolation

Though I hate to cheapen a poem
with slang, it needs to be said
that our brief time together
went straight to video,
though when it was shown at the Odeon
one hot night in Weston-super-Mare,
by mistake, there was a standing ovation
while up in Redcar two misfit teenage girls
had seen it so often
you could see their mouths move in unison,
overdubbing our half-hearted sweet-talk
as they watched it for the sixty-third time.

Weathergirl

In this horizontal, dim-lit world of bed, your feet
become redundant, though we might fit
curtain-rings onto your big toes, bonny girl,
and between them, run a string of drying hams.
There's just enough space in between your knees
for a stout school ruler, with which to measure
the lore of trees and the coming of summer.
But here's where only my tongue will go:
only my tongue and the electrical storm
drifting down from the north. Miracle weather.

Priapus

Year in, year out, I catch myself at it:
quelling the candle, drawing down the smalls
of the latest literary starlet,
crushing them into a soft, white ball

I launch into a corner. Deep in the carpet,
the dust mites, to whom I am God of Virility,
gaze upwards gladly at this cotton comet
which guarantees a season of fertility.

Higher Still

Then let this be our new curriculum:

the zooming-in of grainy flesh
on the lady dentist's drilling arm;

the oxymel of truth and sweetness
we spoon into our children's ears;

not shy first loves, but the chestnut tree
they sit beneath in proper songs;

not the chicaning of a mountain hare,
but the condor's shadow darkening its back.

The Shortcut

On a summer day like this, you pay
for the delicious pleasure
of finding and taking a shortcut:

someone's little finger
will turn up in the heap
in the Used Tickets canister;

there will be the five wild faces
of the Matriani sisters
in the bay window of the bedlam;

news will reach you
of the death of a horse
you once rode across a burning field.

Song

I can no more be your fleece
    than fill the cup of longing
and since we have no gripping talk
    then grip is all our wooing
so slip one hand inside of mine
    and leave it there till morning
your left hand does not need to know
    what my right hand is doing

Song

If it were only in a crowd I'd lost you:
among the runners racing for a train,
the gangs of gleaners cutting through the pasture
at nightfall with their wagons full of corn
or in the swarm of suitors who surround you
or in the banks of clouds which bring the rain
which turns to torrents, rakes and swells the river.
For if I'd lost you thus, I might have found you
instead of knowing this – you're lost forever
and the actors who will play us not yet born.

Escher

Life spoils us with a choice of unfortunate combinations –
a dish of curried eggs, say, or being Italian Glaswegian
but nothing comes close to drunk sex in the early hours,

as I play your pale flanks with kisses, my breath sour
as I lap at the small of your back then dip up to whisper
buttercup at your ear, not yet knowing who you are:

a face on the dawn train or the girl in that print by Escher
who leans from her window and gazes down at the sky
while the townsfolk mind their business miles above her.

The Wish

Yes, I think I would feel better
if they named a rose after me
or a far-flung star
in a seamless solar system,
if my thorns could snag
the fleshtone tights of a dithering gardener,
a teatime sky above her, the reek of hydrogen,
ten little planets swooning in their orbits.

The Wager

Of three things you can be certain:
that four out of five will misspell
the word misspell, that the gravedigger
leaning on a frost-rotten fence
will be rolling a thin cigarette
and that, when at last you come,
I will still be this slow god
from the back of the class, yawning,
just getting around to naming things.

One Thing I Do Know

...my death will not be natural,
there will be no heartstruck crumple,
no handfuls of gaudy capsules,
no redhead nurse, no chemo, no coma.
The blades of a helicopter will spin
my blood across a barley field;
a firing squad will pepper my chest
for someone else's sin.
Lightning will strike or a rare shark
yank me under. May a little Turk,
whose nose I've just broken,
fix me to the wall with a meat knife.
That's the way to end a life
like mine. May my wild-eyed mother
count a dozen women at my grave,
their plump arms round each other.

Intramuros

She lies in her grand apartment
above the spick and span cathedral
in the heart of the walled village
above Manila Bay and she dreams
of the great, ruined cities of Europe:
Vienna crumbling into the ocean,
Warsaw in a plague of frogs and flies,
Lisbon, glimpsing in a fuzz of smoke
and London, where all the black men
have learned to talk like white men,
where all the white men have begun
to talk like these cartoon characters
warming their three-fingered hands
around a bonfire made of love letters.

Simpatika

No one speaks more quietly than the lift girl
rising and descending in the library
at the University of Santo Tomas
whose whisper exists at one scintilla –
no more – above the effort of my silence,
whose words sound like tiny bubbles bursting.
Listen now – a stopped clock has more music,
a tray of water roars and rises higher
and yet when I lean in to choose a number,
I'm certain it is your name she is saying.

The Drop of a Hat

After some months of indecision,
Sykes decided to do his dissertation
on those events which actually had
occurred 'at the drop of a hat'.
He came across a minor skirmish
in the Netherlands War of Independence
caused when an insubordinate colonel
tossed a general's cap in the mud
and then discovered the 400 yards hurdles
at the 1904 St Louis Olympics
was started with the drop of a beret
when the starting gun had stuttered
but that was pretty much the limit,
his paper was returned, marked 'without merit'
though Sykes was later to fall for and marry
a girl who appeared as if from nowhere
and bumped him squarely into the gutter
while chasing her bonnet down Market Street.

from

THE BOOK OF LOVE

(2000)

Happiness is the only sanction of life; where happiness fails, existence remains a mad and lamentable experience.

GEORGE SANTAYANA, *The Life of Reason*

You're never happy unless you're miserable.

MY MOTHER *(to me)*

Incident in a Filing Cupboard

Thank you, she says, *we both needed that*,
as if an intimacy had just occurred between us.
Old so-and-so really blew his top today, I say.
It was always going to happen, she replies.

Unless I've blacked out for a moment or two,
nothing has changed, although I am aware
of an oil-film on my lips, as if I have woken
in the arms of someone entirely unknown.

The female thigh begins a steady atrophy
from the late twenties. *These things happen.*
Male muscle tissue slackens and weakens
from 23. *I always have trouble with figures.*

It's difficult, with both of us seeing people.
One in seven of us doesn't have the father
we think we have. Only 9% of what we say
is understood in exactly the way we mean it.

Where do we go from here? That question!
I offer her a sheaf of processed application forms
like a bouquet. *All these numbers*, I say, as if
the intimacy between us had never taken place.

Because

...you write *yes* a thousand times
on the dry stone wall of me,

embroider a silver lining
in the black cloud of me,

seek out the rescue ship
through the cold lens of me,

delve deep for a lucky dip
in the sand-barrel of me,

speak your name aloud at the end
of the silent film of me;

because each day you remind me
I am the last man alive.

An Older Woman

Mid-1990s, Scotland, dead of winter
And more than old enough to be my mother.
She hailed a taxi in the city centre,
Dropped me off a hundred yards before her
And we were naked fifteen minutes later;
A Brookes & Simmons dress, her bra and knickers
Were delicate and in contrasting colours.
I didn't stop to think if there were others,
Responded prompt and proudly to her orders.
And now I wish to speak to celebrate her
Although I don't know anything about her
Except the spray of freckles on her shoulders
And that she said the world revolved around her.
I know exactly what to do without her.

Love's Young Dream

A snowball's chance in hell was what the guys
At work said. Right enough, she had the pick
Of any man in town. But what the heck,
I thought: faint heart, fair maid and all that jazz.
You've got to try. You never know your luck.
But when I called her up, she wasn't in.
I left a message on her answer-phone:
Black Bo's, I said, tonight at nine o'clock.
I splashed on Gio, creased my 615s
And gelled my hair up in an Elvis lick.
I strolled along the Cowgate and arrived
Bang on, and at the window table, there
She was! And with her, giving me the wink,
The Jewish pope, the constipated bear.

Piquant

Just as, surely, sweat is consommé
or scallions scowled in a jelly-pan
or golden acid, wrathful in a stoppered jar

and other body fluids I shan't mention
are sulphur, globster, stinkhorn, horse or Brie,
then there are these late-on summer days

when, just where nostril meets the upper lip,
a film appears, part sweat, part oil
with a perfect, clean white chocolate smell,

two parts ginger to ninety eight parts milk
and which, when I lean in to take this kiss,
says *fool for sugar*, says *mammals one and all,*

says *never again a love like this.*

Always

After the full-day's westward drive you find
the house familiar from a photograph,
its brass-hung door thrown wide.

A meeting party welcomes you: up front,
the matriarch, corn hair tied in a bunch,
the husband of few words

and, in behind two sniffly, smutty boys
you'll take a good few days to tell apart,
a gran'ma, blunt and blouse.

It's then you sense her, in and down the hall,
so vague, at first you take her for a shadow
or portrait on the wall,

the daughter who, that night, will steal in slow
to visit you with kisses coarse and sweet,
to gift you with her heat,

and who through the remainder of the week
won't speak again, although you send her notes,
whose name you never know.

And always this will whittle at your wits –
the way she gave her nightdress to the floor,
one finger to her lips

to call aboard the silence of the land
to forge the night-time colours in her hair –
until you grow unsure

of what was real and what was in the wind,
of all that being meant before and since
that single word she said.

Marmalade

As some are fooled by twenty words for snow
or think of thunder as a god's complaint,
she'll misinterpret what I'm doing now.

Mind you, it *feels* that good, for her at least,
this dog-watch dalliance, this matinée
performance of our beastly cabaret,

where cupidons join hands around the bed,
the beat-box pumping up *The Best of Stax*.
We're puppy lovers, lire millionaires;

her well-thumbed copy of *The Joy of Sex*
lies open, just beyond the underwear
atop the half-sprung jar of marmalade.

And in that moment where she reaches for
the amyl, I'll remember what you said:
don't try too hard. But it's too late by then:

she's too deep in my squiring to assess
my worth. Face facts, I could be anyone.
So, toss a coin on which will happen next

from all the oldest stories in The Book
of Love: sweet zeros, trains will rattle by,
a husband's car will pull into the drive,

we'll turn out to be twins or some such thing;
she'll pair my socks, she'll sigh, she'll wear my ring,
then leave me at the end of Chapter Five.

Sweet dreams. By all of which I mean, beware;
best know just who and where you are and why,
before you dip your fingers in the jar.

The Twelfth Kind

Sometimes, I imagine you
breaking out the baby-oil or bracing
to pull hot wax-strips from your calves,
holding a dress against you at the mirror
to think your thorough body into it,
to see what he might see.

Or else I imagine Judas,
girding the noose-knot or gauging
the staying power of an elder branch,
spending the silver on the finest bandages
to bind away her small, hard breasts,
to take her secret to the grave.

Lithium

Ten years now since I placed it on my tongue
(eight white pills of a multi-coloured thirty-one):
so much chalk-dust bittering my blood
that spasms lifted me clear off the bed.
Now, having dabbled at The World's End,
I lie here with my one-night friend.
While she slips out to pee, I check the drawer
by the bedside for condoms, finding there
instead her labelled box of those
mineral magic circles, a double dose.
Who knows what packages we keep
and carry with us? Now, I cannot sleep
in this ugly pietà, my suffersome jowl at rest
on the miscued curling stone of her breast.

Voyeur

I ask her, what's sexy? *Watching*, she says.
But watching what? Four strangers making love?
No. Seeing what you're not supposed to see?

No. Thrilling yourself in a hall of mirrors?
Glimpsing the ocean? Looking over the edge
and knowing just how easy it would be? *No.*

How about watching our awkward shape hauled
into the net at last? The gup of a toad's throat
springing back into place? *No. Just watching.*

How about watching the foreshore folding
and folding its constant hunch of luck?
The lone, long walker reaching home at last?

No. Watching a bass string throb and settle
at the end of the final song? The island ferry
returning late and empty, bumping the jetty?

The long cosh of a thaw? An advancing swarm?
No. Just watching, she says and stares
as the ocean booms beyond the window.

Her tea-green eyes. Her brazen hair.
The malt-musk of Laphroaig about her mouth.
The rutting motion of the rocking chair.

For the Birds

The whinchat loves the rich brocades
of Holbein's *Duchess of Milan.*

An albatross will stare all day
at the hairy arses of Etty's satyrs.

A keek at Rauschenberg's stuffed goat
has any sparrow creased with laughter.

And *Cornard Wood* by Constable
will keep a sooty tern amused for weeks.

As I peruse the pirls and curls
of your name scribbled a hundred times

on the back of the phone-book, I hear the *woosh*
as the condor swoops from half a mile up.

Against Naturism

I realise it's not all salad sandwiches
at pinewood picnics, endless volleyball.
I've heard the arguments that talk of shame
and how our forebears thought their bodies dirty;
how *we've all got one. Seen one, seen 'em all.*

But it's not for me, beneath my double load
of Calvinist and voyeuristic tendencies.
For me, I have to see the clothes come off:
the way a button's thumbed through cotton cloth –
a winning move in some exotic game

with no set rules but countless permutations –
or how a summer dress falls to the floor
with momentary mass and with a plash
that stirs us briefly as we ply our passion;
a hand pushed through the coldness of a zip,

three fingertips that follow down the spine
to where a clasp is neatly spun undone
amidkiss, by prime legerdemain
and who cares that it happens once in four
and never, never on the first undressing,

it must be better than a foreskin snagged
on gorse thorns or a cold, fat nipple jammed
in the scissor drawer, the bounty and the blessing,
the mystery of nakedness reduced
till on a par with go-go palaces

where goosebumped, grinding strippers strut their stuff
in the birthday clothes of backstreet empresses,
down on a par with the oncologist
who gropes for lumps, the night-morgue man who clips
his nails amongst the naked, bin-bagged stiffs.

So, stranger, what I want to say is this:
if you're to join me in a little sinning
(and this is my place up here on the right),
please understand I'd value some reluctance,
a cold-feet shiver, as in the beginning

when Eve discovered modesty and slipped
in and out of something comfortable.
For there are many ways to skin a cat,
but ours is human nature – things come off
so rarely. Come in. Let me take your coat.

Troilism

I could mention X, locked naked
in the spare room by two so taken
with each other, they no longer needed him,

or Y who, with an erection in either hand,
said she felt like she was skiing,
or Z who woke in a hotel bed in a maze

of shattered champagne glass
between two hazy girls, his wallet light.
Me? I never tried it, though like many

I thought and thought about it
until a small moon rose above a harvest field,
which was satisfying, in its own way, enough.

Proof

When I rest this page (*this* page)
face up on the bathtub lip,
I notice that a streak of sorry water
ups and throughs and greys the paper
till soon these words are gone.

By which we know: a bookie's slip
soaks up a thimble glass of malt;
a playing card, the philtre in a loving cup.
A summons will dry off a gutter,
a manifesto sucks one quart of milk.

Meanwhile, our banns could barely blot
a pity's weight of blood.

Tricks for the Barmaid

'*None of us are the Waltons*, Ricki Lake said that,'
I tell her, as she shuffles piles of change.

'Did you know most 1950s ice-cream vans
played *The Happy Wanderer*?' She blanks me.

'Elvis's last words were *OK, I won't.*' 'And when
will I hear yours?' she asks. We're getting somewhere now.

I do that burning matchstick trick, you know the one.
She polishes the brass taps with a yellow cloth.

I point out cappucino should have double c.
She chalks it in without a second glance at me.

I show my double-jointed fingers, roll my tongue
and puff my cheeks out till they're red and hold my breath

for several minutes. She tips a Smirnoff bottle up
and clips it to the optic. I know all the words

to *Baker Street* and prove it to her. She knocks off
The Scotsman Brain Game puzzle, starts to yawn.

I tell her, 'It's a long day for the devil, love.'
And it's only then I know who she reminds me of:

it's not that girl I saw in a crowd once but that girl
the girl I saw in a crowd once saw in a crowd once. See?

It's only a matter of time before she sleeps with me.

from **Subject Matter**

English

The way she smooths her neck says
I cook linguini with crème fraîche and salmon.

Her one sleeve open at the cuff says
I write to father more than to mother.

The seam down the side of her jeans says
I hold the telephone *like this.*

When, at times, she walks backwards, it means
what do I care about maps and such?

A scuff on the toe of her left shoe says
the storm behind me will one day demand you.

Games

Peekaboo Horsey Horsey Ring a Roses The Farmer's in His Den
In and Out the Dusty Bluebells Dead Man's Fall White Horses
What's the Time Mr Wolf? Tig Stone Scissors Paper Kerbie
Ducks and Drakes Join the Crew Prisoners' Base Hide and Seek
Hopscotch One Touch Tipcat British Bulldog Chappie Knockie
Chickie Mellie Manhunt Knifie Kiss Cuddle or Torture Long
Sighs and Silences Saying Nothing's Wrong Letter Never Sent
Arriving Hours Late Playing with Her Food Darkly Hinting

Modern Studies

The vulture's just a scrap of scrawn and innards
inside the pungent parka of his feathers.

To keep cool, he pisses down his legs;
he lays a single, silver-speckled egg.

A cheese can't be a Camembert until
it's been strained in a peasant woman's smalls.

How Charles and Paul Hatfield made it rain
in the torrid desert, I shall now explain

for facts and facts alone can keep us sane.

Reject the old beliefs and orthodoxies –
the moon is billy-faced, The Truth is pesky.

There's a hay-bale in the boot of every cab
in London. Maoris sailed clean round the globe

ten centuries before Sir Francis Drake.
The mongoose is descended from the snake.

To modern ears, 'Shakespeare' would sound Bostonian
and Burns like a middle-class Mancunian.

Facts, dear children, is the new religion.

The Beginning of the End

When my ex-wife found magnetic north
in my sock drawer,
I forecast the beginning of the end.

She invited over the neighbour who found
the centre of gravity
thumbed below the surface in the sugarbowl.

They phoned the police who very soon
were squeezing a slew
of anti-chaos from a *Fairy Liquid* bottle.

The sniffer dogs weren't far behind them
and made a beeline for
the rug below which lay Grand Unified Theory.

Soon there were swarms of officials
tugging at the missing link,
fingering the blade-sharp end of my Möbius strip.

I knew I'd have their deaths on my conscience
when they opened up
the drying cupboard and found inside

the nine tenths of the iceberg which usually lie
below the water
which I'd been saving for a rainy day.

Acid

'She was right. I had to find something new.
There was only one thing for it.'

My mother told it straight, *London will finish you off,*
and I'd heard what Doctor Johnson said, *When a man is tired*
of London, he is tired of life, but I'd been tired of life

for fourteen years; Scotland, never thoroughly enlightened,
was gathering back its clutch of medieval wonts
and lately there had been what my doctors called a pica

(like a pregnant woman's craving to eat Twix with piccalilli
or chunks of crunchy sea-coal): I'd been guzzling vinegar,
tipping it on everything, falling for women who were

beautifully unsuitable, and hiding up wynds off the Cowgate
with a pokeful of hot chips drenched in the sacred stuff
and wrapped in the latest, not last, edition of *The Sunday Post*

where I read that in London they had found a Chardonnay
with a bouquet of vine leaves and bloomed skins, a taste
of grapes and no finish whatsoever, which clinched the deal.

Scarlet

I think of Bobby Shaftoe, lost at sea,
his buckles snagged on the wreck in the wrack,
Johnny in the ditch, one scarlet ribbon biting his neck,
who never did make it home from the fair,
Tommy Tucker singing the song of a slashed throat
and Boy Blue, found in the haycock, of whom it was said
he looked for all the world like he was sleeping, not dead.

And I think of my friends and of their friends
and theirs, sitting round the tables in Black Bo's,
not one moral left between them and I suppose
that I must soon finish this and join them,
all the things we know but cannot tell each other
about each other in this half-life of secrets,
the summer night music of now and what-comes-next.

An Outlying Station

A sea-fog like gunsmoke was cresting The Sound
and our coffee steam making the van windows misty,
the morning the crew was at last leaving town.

I say *town*, but more like a village with bells on:
the streets full of strays, houses glutted with ghosties
and squash full of fuck-ups, like Scoraig or Findhorn.

The worst part of three weeks spent watching the telly
in the one pub-cum-caff which served home brew like toffee;
a bar-bint called Morvern who gives men the willies.

Three weeks of bad drugs, badass jazz, bad religion,
the same German blonde who came on to me nightly
and clipper-scalped DJs who talked revolution.

Was I really the only one here who owned luggage?
They watched as I loaded it onto the trolley,
half the weight of their spurious, spiritual baggage.

We boarded the train at an outlying station.
I woke on the border of some brand new country;
my forehead was prickly with chill perspiration.

Athena

Some nights, drunk with wisdom, when the moon is high,
I contemplate the work I'll be remembered by –
each image fresh as if I'd forged it yesterday:

the classic airbrush kitsch I called *Long Distance Kiss:*
a girl, high on mascara, smacks her lipsticked moue
against the telephone, the Muse of loneliness;

or the New Man, Michelangeline, in black and white,
whose new-born son is mewing on his sculpted chest:
a luminary nuzzling its satellite

and that blonde who lifts her tennis skirt up to display
one perfect buttock, as round with promise as the planet
which some day soon our children's children must inhabit.

Bellyful

There was Archie Andrews: a ventriloquist's doll
who did his stuff on Fifties wireless shows
while on the arm of Peter Brough (who, if
he saw the irony, would never say so);

Lord Whassisname, that drunk nob with the monocle;
Lambchop, an adolescent sheep-cum-sock
and Orville, a green duck with a line in pathos
a ladies' man might give his right wrist for.

But if you know your history (and I do),
you'll know this belly-talking business goes
a long way back: before they gottled geer,
Enoch of York, it's said, could do an otter

well enough to charm a trout or two,
his left arm wedged into a wad of fur;
Oswin, whose nymphomaniac falsetto
lured his pursuers into an avalanche

and the imprisoned Mary Queen of Scots
who'd slip her puppet Lizzie out a window
and turn the air around Loch Leven blue,
reciting *The Decameron* in French.

Solo

For once, I felt wanted, dead or alive,
the day my fame outgrew the Famous Five.

There came a time I could give no more
to the other guys in the Gang of Four

and I felt the dead weight fall from me
when I unyoked the clowns of the Crucial Three.

I considered all this as I boarded the bus
to quit the town not big enough for both of us.

One eye didn't seem so much to leave behind
as I sped to my job in the kingdom of the blind.

Pagan

Such things occur: I am driving back to Dunbar
when Shelley strips naked in the passenger seat
to show me the Celtic serpent tattoo

which twists all over the pale force of her body,
the forked tongue flicking the down of her belly.
You must put your faith in something, she says.

Yet what has she done but swap one implausible God
for a full menagerie of impossible ones?
What I believe in are those millions of moments

just before the moments when things go wrong.
I tell her of the night I spent in MacDiarmid's bed
at Brownsbank, snow thick for eerie miles each way;

how I lay and imagined him, alight and magisterial,
swaying on the open-topped night bus north through London;
how coals stirred and settled through the hours of dark.

Shelley sighs, says nothing. For the rest of the journey,
there is only the slow pall of the engine,
the occasional cawing of goddesses, the lowing of gods.

Show and Tell

Astrid had brought in an oxhorn
on which a sailor uncle carved her name;

Glen, a singing cricket in a jar.
By and by, the class were introduced

to copper sulphate crystals in a tube,
an urchin shell that still smelt of the sea.

When at last they came to me, my heart
beat like a vulture chick in a wren's egg.

All night long, Jesus had been whispering
the sweet words in my ear, until I knew,

but now I stood, my hands cupped empty,
pearl tears on the red puff of my cheeks;

their laughter booming down the blue hall,
shaking the little coats on their pegs.

Hobbledehoy

The market garden spread back east towards
what locals call The Honky Tonk estate.
There was that catty smell of flowering currant
in low hothouses rowed with red-hot pokers

and crimson ballerinas, dark potting sheds
where bulbs bulged, centred in loam-filled pots.
The sound of horses passing a window there
one night was a trick of stereo – a recent invention.

I stuck to mono and entertained my great aunts
with Bacharach's *I'll Never Fall in Love Again*
and trotted round them, a hand out for my fee.
A mildew foust which hangs calm in the gents

at St James, as I fasten up my spare,
has triggered this and summoned up Balmullo
on long gone Thursday nights. All's well until
this single flashback I cannot account for:

an awkward girl who is coming up by the length
of pleached hedge as I turn from the window
to grasp the tablecloth's end and pull it –
aware that I haven't yet mastered the trick.

The Man I Could Have Been

The man I could have been works for a vital institution, *is* a vital
    institution.
Without him, walls will crumble, somewhere, paint will peel.
He takes a catch.
He is outdoorsy and says *It was a nightmare* and means the traffic.
He's happy to watch a film and stops short of living in one.

The man I could have been owns a Subaru pickup the colour of
    cherry tomatoes.
He's in the black, not in the dark.
His mother is calm.
Women keep his baby picture in the windownooks of wallets.
No one dies on him.

The man I could have been owns bits of clothes not worn by
    uncles first.
He has no need of medicine.
He walks from Powderhall to Newington in twenty minutes.
He plays the piano *a little*.
Without him, havens buckle, sickbeds bloom.

The man I could have been lives locally.
He is quietly algebraic.
Without him, granite will not glister.
And when he sees a crisis, he does not dive in feet first.
He votes, for he believes in their democracy.

The man I could have been has a sense of direction.
For him, it was never Miss Scarlet with the dagger in the kitchen.
He knows his tilth and sows his seed.
He'll make a father.
He is no maven nor a connoisseur.

The man I could have been has a season ticket at Tynecastle.
He comes in at night and puts on *The Best of U2*.
He browses.
He puts fancy stuff in his bathwater.
He doesn't lace up his life with secrets.

The man I could have been was born on a high horse.
He knows the story of the Willow Pattern.
He had a dream last night you'd want to hear about
and remembers the words to songs.
His back is a saddle where lovers have ridden.

The man I could have been has a sovereign speech in him he's
        yet to give.
He might well wrassle him a bear.
He is a man about town.
He has the exact fare on him.
Without him, motley trauma.

The man I could have been, he learns from my mistakes.
He never thought it would be you.
And no one says *he's looking rather biblical.*
He has no need of London
and walks the middle of the road for it is his.

The man I could have been is quick and clean.
He is no smalltown Jesus nor a sawdust Caesar.
Without him, salt water would enter your lungs.
He doesn't hear these endless xylophones.
That's not him lying over there.

Lullaby

Between the rusted anchor and the resting place

between the rattler's rattle and its fangs

between the looming steeple and the steeplechase

between the skyscape and the boomerang

between the drowsy lovers and the living dead

A to L, my love, and M to Z.

Between the tomboy's cartwheel and the carousel

between the crow's nest and the sinking sun

between amanuensis and Emmanuelle

between the cherry-popper and The One

between reveille bugle and the watershed

A to L, my love, and M to Z.

Between the night-path clearer and the highwayman

between audition piece and curtain call

between the spring's first orphan and the searing-pan

between ignition spark and wrecking ball

between the sleeping beauty and the slugabed

A to L, my love, and M to Z.

CAVOLI RISCALDITI

St Andrews

So many years in Edinburgh now.
Look out – it could be 1986,
The day your teens were jettisoned, blown loose;
A rocket stage. Sweat-darkened underarm,
That silver, crooner's shirt you wouldn't dare
Wear nowadays. Two miles along the sands,
You wilded (whistling 'Chariots of Fire'?)
To where she waited, card high, birthday kiss
Beneath the Martyrs' Monument, a rose,
No snub for being late. Whoever finds,
In things to come, new fear or calm or feels
Their own phantasmal future standing close,
Will suffer, if they only look behind,
The feral past, now frothing at their heels.

Grief

I'm being honest now. The billow burst.
For something lost. Invisibled. Let go.
Those beasts which tap the claret of the worst
Excess – so many moths, too many crows,
Fomenting snails. Heart's arrow? Spine-tailed swift.
On Spottiswoode, tail down, a dog fox walks
The line. Buff scavenger. Not like the fox
Which whelmed us, white-napped pup, a birthday gift
For Loki, late one night by Arthur's Seat.
But careful, let's not stray into the sights
Of those who tot up totems, monitor
Contingent fauna. Snuff the light and heat
Of mourning candles. Sleep on it. Sit tight.
Sorrow makes silence her best orator.

Easter

'Thathais a smaodhnaich ort': that's what
I wrote, then with my Braille board, pricked out
Sweet nothings, forcing you to lift a mask
To see me. Things I hid, that you might find
A glyph, a laic vernicle, a thrill,
Enough to break the silence, later on;
Mnemonics for my name, a billet doux
Between the sixth and seventh biscuit down.
You counted days. A card came in the post
Which ganted open blank. You kept the faith,
Not letting go the ghost. Then when at last
I did come, unannounced, to show my face,
My father's coat and my grandfather's case
I stepped in from the cold, a zealot past.

Vena Cava

When fear saw who we were, I'd cornered you;
My knuckles set, sierra by my ear.
Me bleeding keenly, superficial tangs
Which, like us, wouldn't last the week. We froze,
Could go no further, jammed against the door.
What gain is there, years on, in sending this
Back to the heart? My fist dropped in the air,
Became a cooling hand. Call it a draw,
Call it a day. In time, we must have slept.
But some days, even now, I wake to find
Your small hands, fingers knitted on my chest,
Attempting detonation, a revival
Through thinning blood. I shudder for you, lest
This past would hook me then, dead on arrival.

Heatwave

I cannot tell a lie. I cut it down.
It had distracted me for far too long.
I find a card in which she'd written out
Our full names, sham baroque, and underneath
'*Their children*' like a boneyard epithet.
She stopped at two – the second one, a boy
Upon whose name we never could agree.
Years later, on Columbus Avenue,
I shared a sidewalk table with her wraith,
Hung with the sun, a poppet on her knee.
I sank a bitter coffee, tried to up
My temperature. She stared down at her feet.
I tried. I smiled. I fiddled with my cup,
Then rose, cut down to Broadway in the heat.

Reading the Suddenlys

Another hurricane in Hertfordshire
Is hardly ever happening. I sit
In some mock-tudor outrage of a bar
In AL5, a satellite sump town.
Waiting for you to teach your class, I sift
A local rag. I run my finger down
The deaths looking for *Suddenly*. How far
We've blown: doctor of entomology
Moonlighting at the Sunday school, while I've
My doubts on everything except my fear
Of insects, and that chilling wind which scythes
The past. While walking home, it shifts the land
Behind us, comes up close and disappears
When, suddenly, you stop to take my hand.

Making a Mistake

Taking it black, I long for home. *Home* home.
From making it, I'll learn. So I suppose.
So, coming down for capture, I await
The silence / absence quandary. Let's spend
This spell as quarry trading off the terms
Of reference which knowledge will allow.
To start: what happened last time? *All the awe*
In which the tracker lifted up the game,
Through time's rescission, tempered into fear,
Remorse. To follow? *Mere conjecture.* Hear
How quiet it's become, this far from home.
But silence is unthinkable to me.
Then, hear their remnant voices hounding on
This next mistake: the one I turn and see.

Encraty

The past becomes a cache of private porn:
Rasiert. Lustfauste. Schwanger und So Geil.
Or *Honey Before Breakfast, Girls Who Crave.*
Which girl which time? Which added element?
I grace with fetishes and dight with smiles,
Bow down before the yoni, dithering
For traits; what was removed, how we behaved.
But conversation swells out, gathering
Momentum. Work to do. Behind with rent.
I don't remember this – all sweet talk gone.
So hard to lose control, until a palm
Slapshots through years, stings before I've seen it.
Passive for once. Craven, cold-short. I am.
I say a quiet thankyou, and I mean it.

What Happened Next

She said you had to learn to love the cold,
Lay doubled up. In time, of course, I would.
Each night, for exercise in self-control,
She'd limn a filing cabinet which stood
Beside a swimming pool, about to fall,
Had taught herself to freeze it, just a shade
Above the water, let it hang. She made
Fair game of gravity that way. For all
This mastery, I doubt that, had she swapped
The cabinet for us, she could have stopped
What happens next. We go through the routine
Of kiss and count to ten, start wavering...
I haul myself out, thwarted, shivering.
On looking round, she's nowhere to be seen.

Transfiguration

And now might be the time to improvise
With ones who got away – mendacity's
Extravaganza – make the whole thing up,
For making up's the best part anyway.
So here I am, refashioned in the guise
Of Casanova. Hush. The penny drops.
Another and another, till the floor
Is thick with coins. A brand new look of thirst
Envelops me. They hammer at the door.
A host of gumdrops scuffling to be first.
I undress slowly, paddle through the slush
Of money, turn the key, fit for the rush
And nearly yank the door clean off its post,
To find the hallway lit by squalling ghosts.

Square One

I did as I was told. I bowed my head,
Hands clasped, knelt by the lavatory bowl,
And spoke. Sounds like a horror headline now –
'Two five-year-olds were sent alone to shops.'
The way the butcher winked at us, and how
His thumbs-up seemed a fat straw in the wind,
A ruddy imprimatur. If we found
Free hands, we'd yoke them. When my mother said,
'Say a little prayer for Fiona',
It didn't work. Days later, she was dead.
They had to tell me, had to let me thole
My innocence, her absence, let me cry
True tears at last. Catharsis. When I'd stopped,
The kids next door were told I had sore eyes.

Making a Comeback

I'm standing at the window, waiting for
The cloud's half-hunter to unclip the moon,
A pebble yowl, uniquely nondescript,
So this last week's equation stays unsolved
Inside the jotter, sum of many parts.
You found me though and play a small guitar,
Somewhere behind me. I envisage you
Cross-legged at the centre of my room.
Since you have stripped off, I resolve to start
The correlation, shape up things to come,
To pull the wishbone, shed some light on you.
You tell me that your firebrand days have waned;
The night grows hotter. High time you explained
Just where you've been, that brand new heart tattoo.

Digitalis

'Fire!' quoth the fox, as he pissed on the ice –
A cocky runt – unheeding of the lake
An inch below. He wouldn't say it twice:
The fox is taken when he comes to take.
My past freezes beneath me and I skate.
A flabby heart, twelve generations dull,
Thumps hard beneath my coat, disconsolate.
Above, a weather satellite is pulled
Correct in orbit as the payload sets
About its task, an analytical
Disclosure of tomorrow. Don't forget
To wrap up warm, the time of year for gloves
And scarf. Sensing the ice is critical,
I circle one last time for each I've loved.

Making a Getaway

Surprising I should have – now sparks are flying –
The wedding dream at last, four years in coming.
Retreating from the banquet reverie
Where you sit posied on your bridegroom's knee,
Your mother greets me like a long lost son.
Then later, slipped of cream, scuplted in black,
You entertain my audience of one.
The limousine is waiting. Wish me luck:
I've spent so much in planning this escape.
One last embrace, then time for us to step
Across our thresholds. Yes, she's beautiful.
Yes, so are you. I only hope you've kept
The memories, receipts and, most of all,
Your promise of a file inside the cake.

Abacus

...means 'dust' – for once we counted on the ground.
And now I'm standing in the trees between
The banged-up icehouse at the Hermitage
And, moments on, the rock where Agassiz,
A Swiss geologist, came to displace
All former theories on glaciers.
This silence is immaculate. A log
Is carved into a bare-toothed, cartoon fox
For resting on. I'm sweating like a dog.
The unstrung beads of you seem all around;
Cooled vestiges of you. Look at my face,
Know you can count on me. In time you'll learn –
Think of that glacier, biding its time.
Remember you are dust and shall return.

Halfway Across

A week I waited for the call from you.
Now two desk-drumming hours have lapsed, I think
Less of the minutes we were interlinked
Than of those giddy moments halfway through
We spent cut off, when I stood in the hall
And knew the wire dead beneath my feet
Like Blondin crossing the Niagara Falls
Blindfolded, waiting for a breeze to shift,
For balance to indulge me, you to lift
The set and, bidding, opt for Call Repeat
To ring the silence down. I steadied, knelt
To take the thrill of it, the intimate
Exchange you gift me into, and I felt
A pulse: a ripple in the infinite.

Compendium

Let's sum up so far, bring you up to date
With all the latest scores from round the grounds:
In Pelmanism, all these cards face down
Are still for pairing, still to find what fate
Will deal them. And in Kim's Game, here's the tray
Of objects, rearranged, with one removed.
The snail shell's there, the rose... the memory
Is fading fast. In Cluedo, you've accused
Miss Scarlett with the Dagger in the Hall.
It's just a box of clichés, on the shelf –
A bit like all those words of dread that tell
You kick-off in the Game of Life is imminent:
'We really need to talk.' 'There's been an accident.'
'I'd like to play a song I wrote myself.'

Harm's Way

I think I saw her there, it's hard to tell.
You'd think by now I'd know the way she moves;
You'd think I'd understand how daylight gives,
How last-light thrills and fizzles, how nights fall
In much the way a face falls in a crowd
You'd felt yourself a part of, or a tent
Flaps cold and squandered after an event.
I knew I must not call her name aloud
(I knew I'd left a cigarette alight,
A conversation needing turned halfway
through cooking, something I had meant to say
Before but hadn't felt the moment right).
I stayed, as in a lift jammed between floors
Where all stand stunned and waiting for applause.

Making a Scene

...which pans out from a pearl-glossed nail – Marie's –
As she slips back the sac of isinglass
On the Coolbox shelf beside the surplus ice
Below the rows of Bounty, Mars and Twix;
A fingernail, now notice, which reflects
A tall swart-haired girl balanced on her toes
Upon the kerb outside, who holds her keys,
The space-rock fob of which imparts a pulse
Which gives her such occasioned counterpoise
And makes her thin hand shiver. My demands
Are these: that streams must run with dust and hills
Fall flat, that flame must thaw, that suns must freeze
Before I walk abroad in my own scenes,
Before I give an inch to my disease.

Elsewhere Perhaps Later
(on Julia Margaret Cameron's photo-portrait of Ellen Terry)

Poor Psyche, mourning Cupid's vanishment,
You strive to stop the oil-drip halfway down,
Again, again, to cool it with your breath,
To let it land, a splash of birch cologne
Which pearls his cheek. An arm comes flailing up
But you will get there first, to see him lie –
A fall of topmost fruit – those winning hands
Cupped at his hip. Elsewhere perhaps later
A chrysalis will burst; you'll catalyse
The stewardship of one man's loneliness;
The hollow pupa blowing on the branch,
A dozen decades on. What did emerge
Would never reappear. You'd watch it fly
Into the long and drawn net of the sky.

Life Means Life

It never stops – the sickness drumming on.
'The famous ruler of the light of hate'
'The man drunk seven times upon the road':
This nomenclature, these things my names mean.
And time comes when the new friend has to know
The history. And always there's a swap:
A junkie past, a prison spell, a rape,
The starburst deaths of loved ones. All time low.
To think that I once thought the word calamity
Meant knaves and capers. Now, my low celebrity
Is pass-the-pepper tattle for my doctor
At dinner parties. Here's what makes it worse:
I'd take his drugs, but calm's not what I'm after.
Another life is where my life occurs.

Manila

We should not fathom what is new to us
Impatiently, but give it time to cleave
Away our armour of belief. This view
Is the silver, sprawling Bay I must concede
Did not fall from the sky at some point yesterday
Even the battle a century ago
Is a whisker's breadth away in its own history.
Twilit Ermita where the jeepneys roll,
Whose puck-puck car horns forge a constant music
While five floors up, post-cyclone rain
Putters and blurs our terrace swimming pool
Which fails to overspill, though each hot drop
Impacts, imparted to the whole. Nothing is new
Except this sense of nourishment. And you.

Ether

(after Akhmatova)

We cannot find the way to say goodbye:
We square our shoulders but they do not touch
Where darkness drains from woodlands into sea
Between the continents. This sulk and hush
Leads us into a church where we might witness
High songs, bride-lines, dirges, fontanelles
Immersed, all disappearing in this whiteness
Called cyberspace, and I won't know you well
Where I can't see you. Let's instead do this:
We'll sneak among the gravestones of our pasts
With morning breath which heats and clears the mist.
And shall we cut sharp sticks and, in this ether,
As if in snow or sand, draw palaces
Where we might serve ourselves to one another.

What We Became

And so, if each life if has its nightingale
Events, each sense its honey-time, what will
Mine be? And what becomes of us, my girls,
My branch-line stations? For every pearl –
An oyster shucked. The cabbage on the boil
Has been cooked twice, but once was wonderful.
So here's what we became (*the credits roll*):
The apple and the air through which it fell.
The framed print and the pale square on the wall
Which lies beneath. Invention and the wheel.
(*Applause.*) The lost tongue and the useless bell.
The burlesque and the brooding interval
Of silence versus absence. Thirst and thrill.
The spiral and its sister twist of nil.

from

YEAH YEAH YEAH

(1997)

GRANNY: Did you throw a penny in the wishing well?
TODDLER: Yes.
GRANNY: What did you wish for?
TODDLER: To make a big splash.

– overheard at Earlshall Castle, Fife, 1987

They say simple language is ample for the likes of us.
But the problem with those who call a spade a spade is
this: a shovel gets called a spade. A peat paddle, a Scotch
hand or a hod? All spades. A tortoise, a melon and a
kiss stolen from the wigmaker's daughter? You guessed it.
And only the Lord knows what sideshows of sweetness
and atrocity we will crash past as they drag us scream-
ing all the way back to Babel.

CARRICK WILLIS, *The Likes of Us*

Then

For the first time, I listen to a lost
and secret recording of us
making love near-on ten years ago.

I recognise your voice, your sounds,
though if I knew no better,
I could be any man in any room.

After, the rising sounds of rising
and of dressing and once
as you step up close to the deck,

perhaps to pick up shoes, you sing
the chorus of *Sunday Morning.*
I call on you to hurry and we leave.

It does not end then; the tape rolls on.
A few late cars which sigh by
might have passed us walking away

triumphant, unaware we've left behind
this mop and mow mechanism
of silence to which we may never return.

Sunday Morning 2.13 a.m.

What did we ever solve, in this hooked-in corner
of the night? All we could pause to hear
were minimals of sound – a wafer shifting
in the floor-draught, the butter-sucking mouse
poised and looming in its minor world.

The city's cowled quiet now, with shadows
where nothing will move save tensions
in the mood of light. I know of you this way –
folded in the brood of your sleep, far from here
in miles and in years – semi-precious, imprecise.

St Patrick's Day

the 16th – her

A dream ghost in a naval cap
came calling in the night:
'Your father's lost at sea.' Her father,
a shop manager, three years now
in the Garden of Remembrance,
had taken a dinghy out, odd times,
but always had returned safe,
his hair tossed, cheeks too red.
All day, a slight touch of something;
children in next door's garden,
the radio not quite tuned in.
'Lost, but not at sea,' she said
and turned in with some milk
warmed in a pan on the stove.
The usual sleepy half-promises,
the usual almost perfect silence.

the 16th – him

A day to give up sport, perhaps.
The captain bore down on him
in the changing room: 'Things on
your mind?' Indeed. Find time now,
to change this, all subjects. He could
have gone on to the clubhouse,
a row of gold on the drip-plate,
news of wives-to-be, ex-wives-to-be.
The stereo gone on the blink again;
the haw of the kettle – poor man's music.
No longer willing part of any team,
can't be bothered with this whisky.
The TV brays throughout the evening.
In bed, it seems the rain might just
break through. Get up again, take
the third and hottest shower of the day.

the 17th – I

Two journeys which, in joining,
find their sense. They'd started out.
For her, the Sunday papers – him,
some breakfast, late, consolatory.
It's no one's fault. Though she, perhaps,
or he might have given way. Anyhow,
by the fire station, they crash. A moment
of anger before faces are taken in.
Words and details swapped, they end up
taking lunch at The Hound. Mistaking
the spring's false start for summer,
she walks to the car-park in short sleeves,
head full of two glasses of house red.
He's signed the cheque. It's no one's fault
and no one saw it coming. What's lost
but paintwork? This is a good man's day.

the 17th – II

'That second glass!' she says. He drives
and stops to buy her papers, pays again
and brings the only flowers in the shop:
'To say sorry.' But they both know this
apology's a sham. More than meets the eye.
She contradicts and smiles and tilts
her head back on the rest. Back home,
he puts on coffee: 'Place is such a mess!'
But she is reading, not reading, calls back,
'Make it black,' and softly, under breath,
has placed an "and" between their names
to try the sound. Tomorrow's work, still
hours and hours away, and later he will
watch the way her toes move up against
the cushion, feel her hair's weight on
his lap. The stereo works for once.

the 18th – him

The morning's full of must-be-done.
The mooring place – the bed (found
unmade shamefully the night before) –
creaks under double cargo. She is first
to go. He shaves and leaves the mail
unread, his collar button loose beneath
his tie. The weekly pep talk: 'Teamwork!
Keep the spirits up!' And his are flying.
In his desk diary, by the date, he draws
a four-leaf shamrock and a Star of Hope.
The sharp sun through Venetian blinds,
the day's a blur. 'What's with you today?'
He knows, but keeps it to himself for now.
Cross town, the hammers crash, the dents
are taken out. A brand new headlamp
fixed in place. Car, everything, set anew.

the 18th – her

Back home, she draws her work clothes on,
but calls in sick, falls back to sleep.
At noon, she puts her teacup on the floor,
in camisole and leggings, searches through
old piles of photos, cousins' weddings,
father in his army days. The phone rings
and she lets it ring. At last, she finds
the one; she's five then, feeding swans,
her face a promise. Later on, she takes
a slow walk to The Hound and finds
her car. She laughs. The damage done
is minimal. Thus far. This thought
and that thought cross her mind. At sea.
In the doorway of the pub, a sign says,
'Spend St Patrick's Day at The Hound'.
When no one's looking, she pulls it down.

Manners

I'd squirreled them like rations for
emergencies which might yet come:
the protocol of hand on hip,
the solemn rule of thumb
on flesh, quoting the tournure of a breast.

And had there been a thunderstorm,
whisky on ice instead of wine,
some purpose soaking through the hour,
we might have realigned
the courtesy which kept us dry and dressed.

If blame is down to details, if
you're lost, and if thereby it proves
that manners make the man, and not
that fundamental move
which splits the sky, is anybody's guess.

Coming

Outside the cinema, all evening long,
there is a young man waiting on
the girl who isn't coming.

I watch him stand and smoke and weep,
or crouch down, head in hands,
till one last audience files home to sleep.

And only now do I get to thinking
how the tenpenny hole in his trouser-seat, to me,
is the winking light of a buoy at sea

that marks what is hidden
and the way death comes in to land,
perfect and sudden.

364

On the long, last day of my twenties,
I am plugging a quiz machine
in a dark saloon in the Cowgate.

Beside me, a couple are pushing through
that 'for the best' scenario,
tugging each way till the air is static.

She is Australian, weeping, and sports
a navel ring, an anti-symbol,
while he is foppish, hugging, tries too hard.

It is only in the moment of chaos
we realise what the half-moon
is a half of, what our breath is a gulp of.

Later, when they make a film of this,
my character is younger, handsome
and altogether missing from that scene.

Yeah Yeah Yeah

No matter what you did to her, she said,
There's times, she said, she misses you, your face
Will pucker in her dream, and times the bed's
Too big. Stray hairs will surface in a place
You used to leave your shoes. A certain phrase,
Some old song on the radio, a joke
You had to be there for, she said, some days
It really gets to her; the way you smoked
Or held a cup, or her, and how you woke
Up crying in the night sometimes, the way
She'd stroke and hush you back, and how you broke
Her still. All this she told me yesterday,
Then she rolled over, laughed, began to do
To me what she so rarely did with you.

Prayer To Be with Mercurial Women

Let me never have her father
call me, saying how's about
a round of golf? Instead I'll take
the grim, forbidding monster
who inspects me for a crooked
trouser crease. And spare me too
from palmy evenings which sail by
in restaurants, on barstools,
without a storming off or two.
'Darling, you were made for me.'
I pray I'll never hear those words.
I need to feel I'm stealing
love another man would kill for.
When in sleep she curls herself
around me, may she whisper names
that are not mine. I'd prefer
to be the second best she's had.
A curse on mouths which dovetail
as if there'd been a blueprint made:
I'd rather blush and slobber.
And once a month, please let me be
a punchbag. I'll take the blame
for everything: I want to taste
the stinging of a good slap.
I hope I'll find my begging notes
crumpled, torn in half, unread,
and when I phone, I want to hear
an endless sound of ringing.
Help me avoid the kind of girl
who means things when she says them,
unless she's screeching, telling me
exactly what I am. Amen.

Trespass

The sign said PRIVATE PATH and so we veered,
Drawn woken into possibility
Where, fifty yards ahead, it disappeared
In rusty shade below untended trees.
And just around that corner seemed as good
A place as any I might ever find
To hush her and to ask her if she would.
But then I saw him, cowering behind
A fallen oak, his matted, rocking head,
His thorn-stung nakedness. She tugged my hand
And whispered something. Nothing more was said;
We doubled back towards the light. Whose land
It was I couldn't say. But then, who says?
From then, our days were nights, our nights were days.

On a Promise

(an epithalamium)

And if not caution, then its conduit
Is given to the wind. A giddy ship
Of fools and family, rocking loose (to wit,

There's drink and dancing), witness as you slip
The foolish purchase freedom had become.
Then, clutching at complexity, we strip

The willow, strange brutes turning in a hum
Of shuttles, stripped of any code of dress,
And swirling girls who gracefully succumb

To gallivanting into breathlessness.
And in complexity, accessory
To a loom more excessive than this mess

We mimics weave on, a promissory
Rationale emerges (and not by chance,
There's method in this), a necessary

Arrangement we have conjured from the dance
To celebrate that promises are made
And bargained down, from bittersweet advance

To oath of no retreat, that best schemes laid
To last still can, to scold the cynic's tongue.
No one would claim the tune won't be replayed,

That other hearts won't race, bells hang unrung,
But such shapes aren't fashioned to go through
A repetition. Something is begun.

Some things are made just once, and made for you.

Noyade

To start with, the pricey but possible: bottles
of Hennessy XO which we nip down in thimblefuls,
flutes from a twelve year old Krug jeroboam,
a couple of sweet Cuban breezes to loosen the tongue.

A razor of schnapps while the jukebox cranks up,
then the Armalite, tiger-bite, the test-tube traffic light,
the road to Damascus is long, ma cherie, have
another, another, the night is yet young, we must live.

This cider I snitched from the sleeping Medusa,
a sip from the hipflask of Zeus and this wine
from the well at the end of the world and the juice
of the lustberry drizzled in tumblers on spirals of ice.

For our shivers, a fresh mug of maté, a flambé of raki.
To warm us, a mulled mash of apples, salt slammers of tears.
Now the folk of the city are foundered in sleep
we will unwind our fears in this waltz and our turning

will seed a new language, will send off new colours,
will settle a matter of time, hold the floor, hang the walls,
shake the windows and, seeping out into the street,
it will ripple and swell. It will swallow them all.

from St James Infirmly

Danse Macabre

On Princes Street, I catch the eye of Death
Which drops its jaw and scrambles for the list
Of its impending squeezes. Name's not there!
It's horny for me though – I'm just its type.
Down in St James, it sneaks in on my tail
And gets in first when I attempt to pay.
It wants to have its way with me. I guess
I'll crumble after six or seven pints
Of cooking lager, lean to take a kiss
That's silver-cold, that sucks my beery breath
Until I'm cross-eyed from it and Elaine
Suggests an early night might do me good.
'She's right,' Death whispers, looking at the time,
'I've got to have you now. Your place or mine?'

The Game of Eyes

I catch her eye and catch a hailstone, blind,
Which doubles off the snare-skin of my palm.
I clutch the monumental beer glass, find
A custard mantra – 'Yes, I am, I am.'
Once great aunts flicked my lashes, winked and said
The lassies would sweep easily, knocked dead.
Some potion that, that Chalmers aunties cooked –
All right for them, who to a woman looked
Like Riefenstahl was just around the block
To capture them: a female master race
In fading photographs. And now this face
Which measures mine, on forays to the clock:
Albedo of my skimmed irradiance
Already pasteurised with common sense.

A Brief History of Closing Time

A bawl: 'Last orders at the bar now please!'
The Little Death, which isn't, after all,
A pilfered, pushed-for orgasm, still comes
Served in a woman's voice, breathless and drained;
A grand finale cried by ringing bells.
Then, those for whom it's all but over now
Scrabble for coats and drift towards the door,
Exchanging numbers, wiping upper lips.
Tomorrows are proclaimed and boons invoked.
A trail of five pence pieces on the floor;
A Marlboro in an ashtray, thumbed near dead,
Has shed a dozen keen spittles of fire
From which you cannot turn your gaze until
You count them down through transience, to nil.

Corrida

The taxi driver looks up as I pull
The curtains. There's a language that subsides
Like promising young men who thought the bull
Would wait until they aged before their eyes
Were dazzled by the point itself, a tongue
Common enough to disengage the young
And steer them from the ring. Try telling them
That it ends up like this: sickness, mayhem
And soda water – all that you can take –
The red rag soaking into the eye's white
And raging for some sleep as early light
Seeps through the room's red curtains. Crimson lake,
That colour in a childhood paintbox which
I dabbled with and never sensed so rich.

After Entomology

This getting to know you isn't easy,
like fathoming again the difference
between those insects which come in
at the roadside front of the house,
those which appear from a clear
and verdant stasis round the back,

then those which are, at times, found
struggling against the surface tension
in the toilet bowl at the house's centre:
which are entered as Unclassifiable
in my daybook. After entomology,
my two-leggedness, my lax vanity,

my burdened notion of an in-between:
the dark week when the theatre lies
unvisited or those amassed seconds
of radio dead-time, the notes which
skirl ahead while the piper breathes
or treading water, knowing you'll be saved.

Cardinal

To the north
is a dry dock scuppered by rain.

To the south,
there's a hand sticking out of the mud.

To the east
is the lowest point on a plain.

To the west,
you crack open an egg full of blood.

At the centre, your parents attempt to explain
to each other the chances you had.

Infighting

Take this: for nothing here's chiming, vibrating
and all this vainglory and self-deprecating
just goads at the tender parts, gets irritating.

You'll make no advance advocating monopoly
on any vocabulary; even cacophony
needs the needle to make its point properly.

It's true that you find yourself fey and bewitching,
yet always you feel that the itch that you're scratching's
soothed better by far by bravadoes of bitching.

The off-pat flyting, back-biting and threnody
you render and throw up, at will, won't remedy
the rot of your serenading, lute-laden wannabe.

You can't see a barrier without pushing through it;
it's a poor pearl of pathos you don't disintuit
and you now give a doing when once you'd just do it.

You want my advice? Here it is: try removing
the self from your argument – gluts of self-loving
just pudding the gut of whatever you're proving.

That's it on the chin and I'm sure you can take it,
but that shadow you're boxing is me, so please break it
gently. Best wishes, I hope that you make it.

Noah

Think of him balding, burnt with mine-run drink
with sons chewing the bitter stick all day
who bicker through their endless games of *Risk*
and daughters-in-law combing Oxford St
for each last piece of costume jewellery.

Bereft, arthritic, conjured for too long –
before him, on a table, feathers fall
from where, within his buckram fist, he holds
a small, grey bird he tries but can't let fly
which sputters, takes a full half hour to die.

August (and Nothing After)

As I sit on the bus down the curve of The Mound,
I catch the chat of the couple in front:
'I hear that Roddy Lumsden doesn't believe
in the soul,' she says, and shakes her head.
'Worse than that,' says he, 'they say he won't
even entertain the concept of the soul.
Is that no awfy?' I smile my wicked smile.
Then, full of grace, we crosscut Princes Street
where buskers ply their breeze and bile
and lovers cheek each other in the heat.
An old man's coughing by the flower stand.
Two girls drop into Milne's Bar for a beer.
Our flag is flying in a hundred lands.
'The punishment has got to fit the crime.'
And rising up from Easter Road, a cheer
as Hibs go three down just before half-time.

Rogation

I

How might I make sure to avoid
girls called Alison at all costs?

Same goes for any woman whose name
is splendoured in the torch

of a torch song, second-hand:
Joannas, Saras, Carolines.

At any one time, a dozen red-eyed men
somewhere, gulping back the lyrics:

'Forgive me my unworthiness',
'My aim is true.'

II

And how do I come to one like her
whose name seems that

of a masque, a rogation flower
or a next-month's craze,

whose name crosses the floor
in the steps of an implausible dance?

Oh for the dry, dependable glide
of a Morag, Moira, Shona,

now a drink comes down the bar
with my name on it.

The World's End

Supposing you were wrong and I was right,
I was lying through there thinking
of a place where we and the land must part,

of where a child swings on a wire fence
watching, and where might be found
a paperback whodunnit, blown brown,

where a river stalls and seeps into the grass,
where all the footprints lead one way
and no one, on a late shift, stamps your pass,

where a clisp of light in the willow-herb
is what was dropped from the swag
in the chase, or a shred of a Sixties hothouse;

a place some call a border, some an edge,
as if the many missing or a saviour
will rise in welcome when we step over.

Lines to a Missionary

On some dark night, consider this; beware –
your name may be on a menu somewhere.

A little blood will court the nearing barks
of jackals, or an egg-eyed shark

will snoot you in the blackness, homing in
on fine legs, bare and bicycling.

And no one is exempt – these things occur
like so, no matter who you are,

and nothing in the daybooks of the saints,
in *Life and Work* or common sense

will save you from a beast, thought long extinct,
which thinks your throat fit place to sink

its teeth. If chased by hungry crocodiles,
run zigzag, sure, but reconcile

yourself to your position in the chain;
you may escape, but then again

we'll think no less of you for being killed.
The Christian soul is quite inedible

and better ones than you have turned in awe
to tentacle, to lion's claw.

Mercy

And so, on my return, the terrapins,
Two upturned ashtrays farced with viscera,
Are scrabbling at the bathtub's side, par-boiled
And livid, haggling with mortality –
You having gamely carried out your chore,
Though muddling the hot tap and the cold.

Some skin flakes off. We wait a week before
The first succumbs, breaks water belly-up.
Next morning, you are sent to check the tank.
The second peels and pines, pricks you with guilt.
I scour the owner's manual for hints
On mercy killing methods, come up blank.

This calls for some imagination, since,
Too big to flush away, too still alive
For burial, tradition lets us down.
I scoop it out and drop it in a sack,
While you slip out to start the car, and soon
We're driving slowly to the edge of town.

We circle, find a quiet spot – the moon
A single, silent witness to the deed.
It flails, a wriggling terror in my lap.
I settle it shell-up beneath a tyre;
You deftly hold a balance on the clutch,
Accelerate. I listen for the snap.

At first, it won't appear to matter much;
We'll dine out on the story more than once.
The new pair looks much like the tragic one
And, when you tape those labels, Life and Death,
Onto the bath-taps, how we'll stand and laugh,
Though something sharp will snag us, later on.

Beach Ceilidh

(Pictou, Nova Scotia)

Starters it gets you, everything ploughing –
the music – bugger nuance. Later,
refrains may please or pinch you,
performances are chalked against,
you begin to see a difference between
the fiddler with the quiet eye
and the one with the hop-foot.

From there, it steepens or webs out:
a chorus of unwanted effects.
You cry out for someone to rein in the slack.
Warning notes sound from wet block,
bluff and cove, at any island house
or bonfire site; look for the cloy
of sawgrass smoke, the spoor of cans.

When a new beat won't let up, some buff
claims fado, though you reckon rembetiko.
How much of Europe is here tonight,
immigrant, impetuous? And you, and you.

ITMA

Honeymooning couples blithely hanging out
the DO NOT DISTURB or a Cockney shout

of 'Taxi!' Stewed prunes. All worth a giggle
to them then. The belly dancer's wiggle

of plenty, tawny flesh in a sheik's harem.
A gust up a lady's skirt? They'd scream.

The Great War past, that man about to come:
I suppose we must forgive them.

Poor Noel Coward, sainted for his tat:
today we'd hang him high (if that

were not pernicious). Bones through noses,
and flower fairies teasing in the roses,

next to nothing on, a sort of kiddie porn
for aesthetes. The past is thick with corn

we wouldn't touch, we who have premature
nostalgia, a predilection for the pure

emphatics of the recent: a Seventies rich
with pre-modern, post-evolution kitsch

and spells with fever. Easy to get smitten.
The past rolls over, begs to be rewritten.

Stay calm. We've seen the future and its name
is more or less more of the same.

See, there's Strummer kicking in his amp
and, outside, Formby leaning on a lamp.

The Boy

The old men at the gate were whispering
about what colour ink Drew Meldrum's will
was written in, when instinct drew me near.
My mother ushered me towards the door,
repeated what we'd heard and sent me off.

This was in the days when words were currency –
and good ones kept a man in drink for weeks.
My dad would eke out versions of each tale,
a yarn, a shanty, even epic verse
if connoisseurs were lurking in the midst.

I found him in the snug at Guddler Bob's,
his custom tankard raised above his brow,
two just-off-duty barmaids, eyes a-pop
at what I'd heard so many times that week,
I'd cribbed a fledgling version for myself.

He shushed and introduced me as The Boy
and filled his empty nip glass up with beer
and pushed it at me. Being just thirteen,
I sat there sheepish, giving them the eye,
though neither had a second glance for me.

Not yet. But that's how stories often start –
not with a war or witch or blazing tower
but with The Boy sat quiet by a fire
raked down to embers, tempering the powers
that might sustain him on the darkened road.

I listened to each word my father said.
My pulse popped with a courage in my veins:
I knew at last that I could better him
and laden with this knowledge, out I strode
like Hansel with his pocketful of crumbs.

Roisín's Wolves

You lost a pale cheek in their pelts – dark-mouthed, imaginary wolves
you kept about for company while working round the elements
of difference a child must learn to isolate and steer around:
that business of the stalagmites and stalactites; the vagaries
of viaduct and aqueduct; the fickle stings of wasps and bees.
Toughest of all, perhaps, you found gradations of that numb word 'love'
we use too easily and keep dividing and dividing as
is in our brittle way of things.
                              In turn, those wolves will rouse from sleep
you left them to and one will paw the air for you, a hank of sleek
become at last the seeking beast you sensed yet did not understand,
which whines the night, intuiting the loops of truth you must yourself
untie, untie.
            So let them go, the others, find the difference
in reason, sorrow, moonrise, stealth. You must now keep the best of all:
the wolf which knows it best to kill the shepherd first and not the sheep.

The Ultimate Curve

Not even Raphael could draw that scene
(Though sources hint he tried it more than once)
Where Euclid stooped to pull from where it hid
A grandiose parabola. And then
There's Giotto who, it's said, would reach to pluck
A perfect, hand-drawn circle from midair.
That's kids' stuff though. The duodenal dip,
Duomo or the dromedary's back:
No joy. An egg comes close but offers up
Such meagre pleasure. Easy on the eye
Is not what I've in mind – spectacular
And ready-made – which I resolve to file
Beside two other mysteries of life:
Houdini's death, the name of Jack Sprat's wife.

Vanishing

Inside the box, her heels escape the air.
He hears the hollow silence, turns to where
The blades are catching all eyes in the hush.
His click of fingers touches off a rush
Of cymbals. Now he holds the first blade taut
And steers its whetted edge toward the slot.
She slips out of her costume, checks her face
As he reveals the white dove in her place.
She lingers till the last of the applause,
Collects her things, while back on stage he saws
Himself in half with worry, grins with fear.
The sea of faces knows she'll reappear
Amongst them soon. She slams a backstage door.
Her high heels echo in the corridor.

The Answers

'A / B / LOTS OF THINGS'
*(graffito chalked on the pavement
below my bedroom window)*

to talk a good man up into his noose
to watch him swing and cut him loose

to kick down or cross the hurdles of desire
to interrogate the fire

to brink at it, to undiscover thirst
to get there first

to make the soul enter the iron
to play La Cucaracha on my siren

to ache well, walk upon the seven seas
to take my pride to the disease

to walk face up in the limbic storm
to slough my norm

to paint the town with a brushful of blood
to be the millionth customer of love
to have to have

to widen and to wizen
to listen, listen, listen

to be halfway healed and be hunted
to get just what I always wanted

to have you ever in my sights
yes you, to find my name in lights
to get these answers right

to say hello to everyone who knows me
to make the living this world owes me

to rub my salt right in
to win and win

to get down in two, to last
to step aside and let the bullet past

to see the light to be seen in, to rise
to write the rules of compromise

to bust the sacerdotal
to come hither and be total

to be kind to be cruel to my sisters and brothers
to be self-effacing on behalf of others

to hear behind me the soundtrack lurch
to reheat the cabbage, carry a torch

to never accept the nearest offer
to blithely suffer
to beg to differ

to gaze out from the manes of Pegasus
to diagnose the morbus scotticus

to be fair and to be mistletoe
to be necessarily so

to empty the void, to solve the case
of do or die, to spite my face

to borrow the stars from the dark and to keep one
to be a deep one

to see just how much I can take
to guess the weight of the angel cake
to lie back and fake

to dangle my feet in the sky
to say when and know why

to strut my stuff, to repent at leisure
to struggle for pleasure

to unexplain, to whip the core
from the apple, to make the high score

to find the exit in the theatre of passion
to come back into fashion

to look down proud into the cot
to damn well want what I haven't got

to be a proper thorn in the eye
to go forth and multiply
to love, to die.